Interactive Reader and Study Guide

Holt California Social Studies

World History
Ancient Civilizations

HOLT, RINEHART AND WINSTON
A Harcourt Education Company
Orlando • Austin • New York • San Diego • Toronto • London

ISBN 0-03-042088-1

17 18   0982   17 16 15 14 13 12
4500342266

Contents

Contents

Uncovering the Past

ENGLISH–LANGUAGE ARTS STANDARDS
READING 6.1.0 Students use their knowledge of word origins and word relationships, as well as historical and literary context clues, to determine the meaning of specialized vocabulary and to understand the precise meaning of grade-level-appropriate words.

CHAPTER SUMMARY

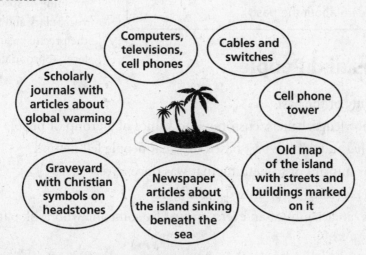

COMPREHENSION AND CRITICAL THINKING

Use information from the graphic organizer to answer the following questions.

1. Explain Did people live on this island before the water covered it?

_____

2. Draw Inferences What was most likely the predominant religion among the people who lived on this island?

_____

3. Identify Cause and Effect What global climatic phenomenon caused the water to rise and cover the island?

_____

4. Evaluate Was the civilization of the island technically advanced?

_____

_____

Uncovering the Past

MAIN IDEAS

1. History is the study of the past.
2. We can improve our understanding of people's actions and beliefs through the study of history.
3. Historians use clues from various sources to learn about the past.

 READING 6.1.0
Students use their knowledge of word origins and word relationships, as well as historical and literary context clues, to determine the meaning of specialized vocabulary and to understand the precise meaning of grade-level-appropriate words.

Key Terms and People

history the study of the past

culture the knowledge, beliefs, customs, and values of a group of people

archaeology the study of the past based on what people left behind

fossil a part or imprint of something that was once alive

artifacts objects created by and used by humans

primary source an account of an event created by someone who took part in or witnessed the event

secondary source information gathered by someone who did not take part in or witness an event

Academic Vocabulary

values ideas that people hold dear and try to live by

Section Summary

THE STUDY OF THE PAST

History is the study of the past. Historians are people who study history. <u>Historians want to know how people lived and why they did the things they did.</u> They try to learn about the problems people faced and how they found solutions. They are interested in how people lived their daily lives. They study the past to understand people's culture. **Culture** is the knowledge, beliefs, customs, and values of a group of people.

The study of the past based on what people left behind is called **archaeology** (ahr-kee-AH-luh-jee).

> What do we call people who study how people lived in the past?
>
> _____
>
> _____

Section 1, *continued*

Archaeologists explore places where people once lived, worked, or fought. They examine the things that people left in these places to learn what they can tell about the past.

> How can studying history teach you about yourself?
> _____
> _____
> _____

UNDERSTANDING THROUGH HISTORY

Understanding the past helps you understand the world today. History can even teach you about yourself. What if you did not know about your own past? You would not know what makes you proud about yourself. You would not know what mistakes you should not repeat.

History is just as important for groups. What would happen if countries had no record of their past? People would not remember their nation's great triumphs or tragedies. History shapes our identity and teaches us the **values** that we share.

History also teaches about cultures that are unlike your own. Learning other people's stories can help you respect and understand different opinions. You also learn to understand how today's events are shaped by events of the past. History encourages you to ask important questions.

> Circle the sentence that explains why history helps you relate more easily to people of different backgrounds.

USING CLUES

We learn about history from a variety of sources. **Fossils**, such as bones or footprints preserved in rock, give us clues to life very long ago. **Artifacts**, such as tools, coins, or pottery, also give us information. Writing has taught us a great deal. Writing can be a **primary source** (by someone who took part in or witnessed an event) or a **secondary source** (information gathered by someone who did not take part in or witness an event).

> What sources give us clues to life very long ago?
> _____
> _____
> _____

CHALLENGE ACTIVITY

Critical Thinking: Drawing Inferences Imagine a tribe or group of people that might have lived a long time ago. Write a short essay about their culture. **HSS Analysis Skills HR 3, HI 1**

Uncovering the Past

MAIN IDEAS

1. Geography is the study of places and people.
2. Studying location is important to both physical and human geography.
3. Geography and history are closely connected.

 READING 6.1.0
Students use their knowledge of word origins and word relationships, as well as historical and literary context clues, to determine the meaning of specialized vocabulary and to understand the precise meaning of grade-level-appropriate words.

Key Terms and People

geography the study of the earth's physical and cultural features

environment all the living and nonliving things that affect life in an area

landforms the natural features of the land's surface

climate the pattern of weather conditions in a certain area over a long period of time

region an area with one or more features that make it different from surrounding areas

resources materials found in the earth that people need and value

Academic Vocabulary

features characteristics

Section Summary

STUDYING PLACES AND PEOPLE

To understand what happened in the past, you need to know where events took place and who was involved. That is why historians study the earth's physical and cultural **features**, such as mountains, rivers, people, cities, and countries. This study is called **geography**.

Geography has two main areas of study. Physical geography is the study of the earth's land and features. Human geography is the study of people and the places where they live. Physical geographers study the **environment**, which includes all the living and nonliving things that affect life in an area. The most important features for physical geographers are **landforms**, the natural features of

What subject helps historians to understand where events took place?

_____

_____

What are the two main areas of study in geography?

_____

_____

_____

the land's surface. Physical geographers also study **climate**, the weather conditions in a certain area over a long period of time. Specialists in human geography study many interesting questions about how people and the environment affect each other.

> **What is climate?**
> _____
> _____
> _____

STUDYING LOCATION

No two places are exactly alike. That is why geographers try to understand how different locations can affect human populations, or groups of people. Geographers use maps to study and compare locations. A map is a drawing of an area. Some maps show physical features, such as mountains, forests, and rivers. Other maps show cities and the boundaries of states or countries. Studying location is often helped by learning about **regions**, or areas with one or more features that make them different from surrounding areas.

> **What is the main tool that geographers use to study and compare locations?**
> _____
> _____

GEOGRAPHY AND HISTORY

Geography gives us important clues about the people and places that came before us. Like detectives, we can piece together a great deal of information about past cultures by knowing where people lived and what the area was like.

> **Underline the sentence that explains how geography gives us clues about the past.**

Early people settled in places that were rich in resources. **Resources** are materials that are found in the earth that people need and value. Resources include water, animals, land for farming, stone for tools, and metals. Features and resources influence the development of cultures and the growth of civilizations. The relationship between geography and people is not one sided. People influence their environments in both positive and negative ways.

CHALLENGE ACTIVITY

Critical Thinking: Drawing Inferences Draw a map of an imaginary country or region. Include features such as mountains, rivers, and cities.
HSS Analysis Skills CS 3

Name _____ Class _____ Date _____

The Stone Ages and Early Cultures

HISTORY-SOCIAL SCIENCE STANDARDS
HSS 6.1 Students describe what is known through archaeological studies of the early physical and cultural development of humankind from the Paleolithic era to the agricultural revolution.
HSS Analysis Skill HI 1 Explain central issues and problems from the past.
HSS Analysis Skill HI 2 Understand and distinguish sequence.

CHAPTER SUMMARY

Need for food	led to	**development of tools**
Changes in climate patterns	led to	**migrations**
Need to communicate	led to	**development of language**
Farming communities	led to	**growth of towns**

COMPREHENSION AND CRITICAL THINKING

Use information from the graphic organizer to answer the following questions.

1. Explain What were the earliest stone tools used for?

_____

_____

2. Identify Cause and Effect Why did so many people migrate during the ice ages?

_____

_____

3. Evaluate Why did hunter-gatherer societies develop language?

_____

4. Draw a Conclusion How did farming contribute to the growth of towns?

_____

_____

Interactive Reader and Study Guide

The Stone Ages and Early Cultures

MAIN IDEAS

1. Scientists study the remains of early humans to learn about prehistory.

2. Hominids and early humans first appeared in East Africa millions of years ago.

3. Stone Age tools grew more complex as time passed.

4. Hunter-gatherer societies developed language, art, and religion.

 HSS 6.1

Students describe what is known through archaeological studies of the early physical and cultural development of humankind from the Paleolithic era to the agricultural revolution.

Key Terms and People

prehistory the time before there was writing

hominid an early ancestor of humans

ancestor a relative who lived in the past

tool any handheld object that has been modified to help a person accomplish a task

Paleolithic Era the first part of the Stone Age

hunter-gatherers people who hunt animals and gather wild plants, seeds, fruits, and nuts to survive

society a community of people who share a common culture

Academic Vocabulary

distribute to divide among a group of people

Section Summary

SCIENTISTS STUDY REMAINS

Although humans have lived on the earth for more than a million years, writing was not invented until about 5,000 years ago. Historians call the time before there was writing **prehistory**. To study prehistory, historians rely on the work of archaeologists and anthropologists.

Archaeologists have found fossil bones that appear to belong to early **hominids**, early **ancestors** of humans. Discoveries of ancient bones give us information about early humans and their

> **What do historians call the time before there was writing?**
>
> _____
>
> _____

ancestors, but not all scientists agree on the meaning of these discoveries.

HOMINIDS AND EARLY HUMANS

As time passed hominids became more like modern humans. Many scientists think that the first modern humans appeared in Africa about 200,000 years ago. Scientists call these early humans *Homo sapiens*, or "wise man." Every person alive today belongs to this group.

> What do scientists call modern humans?
> _____
> _____

STONE AGE TOOLS

During the **Paleolithic** (pay-lee-uh-LI-thik) **Era**, which lasted until about 10,000 years ago, people used sharpened stones as **tools**. Stone tools were probably used to cut, chop, and scrape roots, bones, or meat. Later, people learned how to attach wooden handles to sharp stones to make hand axes and spears.

> What is an advantage of attaching a wooden handle to a stone tool? Draw a picture if it will help you visualize the tool.

HUNTER-GATHERER SOCIETIES

Anthropologists believe that early humans lived in small groups of **hunter-gatherers**. In these **societies**, men hunted and women collected plants to eat and took care of children. These societies developed cultures with language, religion, and art. Language developed as a means of communicating and of resolving issues like how to **distribute** food.

> What cultural element did Stone Age societies develop as a means of communicating and resolving issues?
> _____
> _____

CHALLENGE ACTIVITY

Critical Thinking: Drawing Inferences Many years from now, an archaeologist discovers your house with nothing in it but old furniture, appliances, tools, and bits of clothing. Write a short essay describing some conclusions the archaeologist might draw from these artifacts.
HSS Analysis Skills HR 3, HR 5, HI 4

The Stone Ages and Early Cultures

MAIN IDEAS

1. People moved out of Africa as the earth's climates changed.
2. People adapted to new environments by making clothing and new types of tools.

 HSS 6.1

Students describe what is known through archaeological studies of the early physical and cultural development of humankind from the Paleolithic era to the agricultural revolution.

Key Terms and People

ice ages long periods of freezing weather

migrate move to a new place

land bridge a strip of land connecting two continents

Mesolithic Era the middle part of the Stone Age, from about 10,000 years ago to about 5,000 years ago

Section Summary

PEOPLE MOVE OUT OF AFRICA

About 1.6 million years ago, many places around the world began to experience **ice ages**, or long periods of freezing weather. In response to these changes, many hominids **migrated** from Africa to Asia and eventually spread to India, China, Southeast Asia, and Europe. The ice ages ended about 10,000 years ago.

During the ice ages, huge sheets of ice covered much of the earth's land. These ice sheets were formed from ocean water, leaving ocean levels lower than they are now. Many areas that are now under water were dry land then. Scientists think that in some places the ocean level dropped and exposed **land bridges** between continents. These land bridges allowed Stone Age people to migrate around the world. Early humans probably came to North America across a land bridge from northern Asia, and spread throughout North America and to South America. By 9000 BC, humans lived on all continents except Antarctica.

From which continent did the first early humans probably come to North America?

_____

_____

PEOPLE ADAPT TO NEW ENVIRONMENTS

Early people had to learn to adapt to new environments. The places to which they migrated were often much colder than the places they left, and often had strange plants and animals.

To keep warm, they learned to sew animal skins together to make clothing. At first they took shelter in caves. When they moved to areas with no caves, they built their own shelters. At first these shelters were pits in the ground with roofs of branches and leaves. Later, people learned to build more permanent structures with wood, stone, clay, or other materials, even bones from large animals such as mammoths. They covered frames with animal hides to form solid roofs and walls.

> What materials did early humans use to cover frame structures with roofs and walls?
> _____
> _____

People also began to make new types of tools. These tools were smaller and more complex than tools from the Paleolithic Era. They defined the **Mesolithic** (me-zuh-LI-thik) **Era**, which began more than 10,000 years ago and lasted to about 5,000 years ago in some places. These new tools included hooks and spears for fishing, and bows and arrows for hunting.

People in the Mesolithic Era also developed new technologies to improve their lives. For example, they learned how to make pots from clay, how to hollow out logs to make canoes, and how to use dogs for protection and to help them hunt.

> How did early humans make canoes?
> _____
> _____
> _____

CHALLENGE ACTIVITY

Critical Thinking: Drawing Inferences Draw a building plan with written instructions for a Mesolithic dwelling. **HSS Analysis Skills HI 1, HI 3**

The Stone Ages and Early Cultures

Section 3

<table>
<tr><td>

MAIN IDEAS

1. The first farmers learned to grow plants and raise animals in the Stone Age.

2. Farming changed societies and the way people lived.

</td></tr>
</table>

 HSS 6.1
Students describe what is known through archaeological studies of the early physical and cultural development of humankind from the Paleolithic era to the agricultural revolution.

Key Terms and People

Neolithic Era the last Stone Age, lasting from about 10,000 years ago to about 5,000 years ago in Egypt and Southwest Asia and later elsewhere

domestication the process of changing plants or animals to make them more useful to humans

agriculture the development of farming from the domestication of plants

megaliths huge stones used as monuments or sites for religious gatherings

Academic Vocabulary

development creation and growth

Section Summary

THE FIRST FARMERS

A warming trend brought an end to the ice ages, and new plants began to grow in some areas. As early as 10,000 years ago, in Egypt and Southwest Asia, people came to depend on wild barley and wheat for food. People soon learned that they could plant seeds to grow their own crops. This shift from food gathering to food producing defined the **Neolithic** (nee-uh-LI-thik) **Era.**

This **domestication** of plants led to the **development** of **agriculture**, or farming. The first farmers also learned to domesticate animals. Instead of following wild herds, they could now keep sheep and goats for milk, food, and wool. People could also use large animals like cattle to carry loads or to pull large tools used in farming. Domestication

> **What brought an end to the ice ages?**
>
> _____
>
> _____

> **Use the library or an online resource to find a map showing where specific plants and animals were first domesticated.**

Interactive Reader and Study Guide

greatly improved people's chances of surviving. With survival more certain, people could focus on activities other than finding food.

During this time, people also learned to polish stones to make specialized tools like saws and drills. People also learned how to make fire. Before learning that skill, people could use only fire that had been started by natural causes, such as lightning.

> **What great discovery did Neolithic people make about fire?**
> _____
> _____
> _____

FARMING CHANGES SOCIETIES

People began to make clothing from plant fibers and wool as well as from animal skins. As these early farmers learned to control their own food production and to make better shelters and clothing, populations grew. In some areas farming communities developed into towns.

> **What materials were first used by Neolithic people to make clothing?**
> _____
> _____
> _____

Some groups gathered to perform religious ceremonies around huge stone monuments called **megaliths**. These people probably believed in gods and goddesses associated with the four elements—air, water, fire, and earth—or with animals. Some scholars believe that prehistoric people also prayed to their ancestors. Some societies today still hold these beliefs.

> **What are the four elements?**
> _____
> _____
> _____
> _____

CHALLENGE ACTIVITY

Critical Thinking: Drawing Inferences Use the Internet or a library to research theories about how the megaliths at Stonehenge in England were built. Then write your own theory. **HSS Analysis Skills HR 1, HR 4, HR 5, HI 5**

Mesopotamia and the Fertile Crescent

HISTORY–SOCIAL SCIENCE STANDARDS
HSS 6.2 Students analyze the geographic, political, economic, religious, and social structures of the early civilizations of Mesopotamia, Egypt, and Kush.
HSS Analysis Skill CS 3 Use maps to identify physical features.

CHAPTER SUMMARY

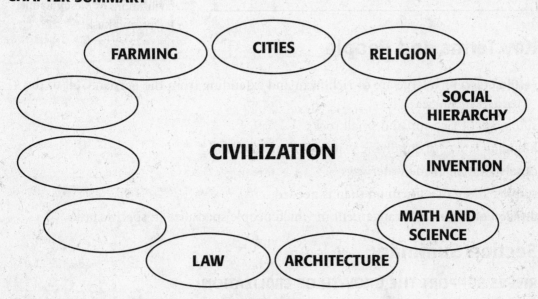

COMPREHENSION AND CRITICAL THINKING

Use information from the graphic organizer to answer the following questions.

1. Identify Which two of the eight aspects of civilization in the graphic organizer above can be classed as economic structures?

_____

_____

2. Interpret Of the following five words (ARTS, SILT, WRITING, TRADE, OIL), which three belong in the graphic organizer above? Write the three correct words in the empty circles.

3. Sequence Of the eleven words or phrases around the word CIVILIZATION, which comes first in time order? Which do you think comes last?

_____

_____

Mesopotamia and the Fertile Crescent

MAIN IDEAS

1. The rivers of Southwest Asia supported the growth of civilization.
2. New farming techniques led to the growth of cities.

 HSS 6.2
Students analyze the geographic, political, economic, religious, and social structures of the early civilizations of Mesopotamia, Egypt, and Kush.

Key Terms and People

Fertile Crescent a large arc of rich farmland extending from the Persian Gulf to the Mediterranean Sea

silt a mix of rich soil and small rocks

irrigation a way of supplying water to an area of land

canals human-made waterways

surplus more of something than is needed

division of labor an arrangement in which people specialize in specific tasks

Section Summary

RIVERS SUPPORT THE GROWTH OF CIVILIZATION

Early people settled where crops would grow. Crops usually grew well near rivers, where water was available and regular floods made the soil rich.

Mesopotamia, part of the region known as the **Fertile Crescent** in Southwest Asia, lay between the Tigris and Euphrates rivers. Every year, floods on the rivers brought **silt**. The fertile silt made the land ideal for farming.

> "Mesopotamia" means "between the rivers" in Greek. To which two rivers does the name of the region refer?
>
> _____
> _____
> _____

Hunter-gatherer groups first settled in Mesopotamia more than 12,000 years ago. Over time these people learned how to work together to control floods. They planted crops and grew their own food.

Farm settlements formed in Mesopotamia as early as 7000 BC. Farmers grew wheat, barley, and other grains. Livestock, birds, and fish were also sources of food. Plentiful food led to population growth and villages formed. Eventually, these early villages developed into the world's first civilization.

> Name two grains grown by Mesopotamian farmers.
>
> _____
> _____
> _____

FARMING AND CITIES

Early farmers faced the challenge of learning how to control the flow of river water to their fields in both rainy and dry seasons. Flooding destroyed crops, killed livestock, and washed away homes. When water levels were too low, crops dried up.

> Underline the sentence that lists some of the problems caused by flooding.

To solve their problems, Mesopotamians used **irrigation**. They dug out large storage basins to hold water supplies. Then they dug **canals** that connected these basins to a network of ditches. These ditches brought water to the fields and watered grazing areas for cattle and sheep.

> From where did the water collected in the storage basins come?
> _____
> _____

Because irrigation made farmers more productive, they produced a **surplus**. Some people became free to do other jobs. For the first time, people became craftspersons, religious leaders, and government workers. A **division of labor** developed.

Mesopotamian settlements grew in size and complexity. Most people continued to work in farming jobs. However, cities became important places. People traded goods in cities. Cities became the political, religious, cultural, and economic centers of Mesopotamian civilization.

> Which places in Mesopotamia became the centers of civilization?
> _____
> _____

CHALLENGE ACTIVITY

Critical Thinking: Drawing Inferences Write a proposal for an irrigation system that will divert flood waters and benefit riverbank farmers.
HSS Analysis Skills HI 2, HI 6

Mesopotamia and the Fertile Crescent

MAIN IDEAS

1. The Sumerians created the world's first complex, advanced society.

2. Religion played a major role in Sumerian society.

3. Sumerian society was divided into classes.

 HSS 6.2

Students analyze the geographic, political, economic, religious, and social structures of the early civilizations of Mesopotamia, Egypt, and Kush.

Key Terms and People

rural having to do with the countryside

urban having to do with the city

city-state a political unit consisting of a city and the surrounding countryside

empire land with different territories and people under a single rule

polytheism the worship of many gods

priests people who performed religious ceremonies

social hierarchy a division of society by rank or class

Academic Vocabulary

role a part or function

Section Summary

AN ADVANCED SOCIETY

In southern Mesopotamia about 3000 BC, people known as the Sumerians (soo-MER-ee-unz) created a complex, advanced society. Most people in Sumer (soo-muhr) lived in **rural** areas, but they were governed from **urban** areas that controlled the surrounding countryside. The size of the countryside controlled by each of these **city-states** depended on its military strength. Stronger city-states controlled larger areas. Individual city-states gained and lost power over time.

Around 2300 BC Sargon was the leader of the Akkadians (uh-KAY-dee-uhns), a people who lived to the north of Sumer. Sargon built a large army

> ① Why do you think governments are usually located in cities?
>
> governed from urban areas that controlled

and defeated all the city-states of Sumer as well as all of northern Mesopotamia. With these conquests, Sargon established the world's first **empire**. It stretched from the Persian Gulf to the Mediterranean Sea. The Akkadian empire lasted about 150 years.

> Use a world atlas to determine how many miles across the Akkadian empire extended.

RELIGION SHAPES SOCIETY

Religion played an important **role** in nearly every aspect of Sumerian public and private life. Sumerians practiced **polytheism**, the worship of many gods. They believed that their gods had enormous powers. Gods could bring a good harvest or a disastrous flood. The gods could bring illness or they could bring good health and wealth. The Sumerians believed that success in every area of life depended on pleasing the gods. Each city-state considered one god to be its special protector. People relied on **priests** to help them gain the gods' favor. Priests interpreted the wishes of the gods and made offerings to them.

> ② Do you think religion plays an important role in public life today? Why or why not?
>
> _____
> _____
> _____
> _____

A **social hierarchy** developed in Sumerian city-states. Kings were at the top. Below them were priests and nobles. The middle ranks included skilled craftspeople and merchants. Farmers and laborers made up the large working class. Slaves were at the bottom of the social order. Although the role of most women was limited to the home and raising children, some upper-class women were educated and even became priestesses.

> 3 In Sumerian religious practice, what did priests do to try to please the gods?
>
> _____
> _____

> 4 Which two groups formed the Sumerian upper classes?
>
> _____
> _____
> _____

CHALLENGE ACTIVITY

Critical Thinking: Drawing Inferences You are a servant to the king of a Sumerian city-state. Write down an account of the king's instructions to the city's priests asking them to make offerings to the gods in order to protect the farms from a possible flood. **HSS Analysis Skills HI 1, HI 4**

Mesopotamia and the Fertile Crescent

MAIN IDEAS

1. The Sumerians invented the world's first writing system.

2. Advances and inventions changed Sumerian lives.

3. Many types of art developed in Sumer.

 HSS 6.2
Students analyze the geographic, political, economic, religious, and social structures of the early civilizations of Mesopotamia, Egypt, and Kush.

Key Terms and People

cuneiform the Sumerian system of writing, which used symbols to represent basic parts of words

pictographs picture symbols that represented objects such as trees or animals

scribe writer

epics long poems that tell the story of a hero

architecture the science of building

ziggurat a pyramid-shaped temple tower

Section Summary

THE INVENTION OF WRITING

The Sumerians made one of the greatest cultural advances in history. They developed **cuneiform** (kyoo-NEE-uh-fohrm), the world's first system of writing. But Sumerians did not have pencils, pens, or paper. Instead, they used sharp reeds to make wedge-shaped symbols on clay tablets.

Sumerians first used cuneiform to keep records for business, government, and temples. As the use of cuneiform grew, simple **pictographs** evolved into more complex symbols that represented basic parts of words. Writing was taught in schools. Becoming a writer, or **scribe**, was a way to move up in social class. Scribes began to combine symbols to express complex ideas. In time, scribes wrote works on law, grammar, and mathematics. Sumerians also wrote stories, proverbs, songs, poems to celebrate military victories, and long poems called **epics**.

> Write the name of the world's first system of writing.
> _____
> _____

> What are pictographs?
> _____
> _____
> _____
> _____

Interactive Reader and Study Guide

ADVANCES AND INVENTIONS

The Sumerians were the first to build wheeled vehicles like carts and wagons. They invented the potter's wheel, a device that spins wet clay as a craftsperson shapes it into bowls. They invented the ox-drawn plow and greatly improved farm production. They built sewers under city streets. They learned to use bronze to make strong tools and weapons. They named thousands of animals, plants, and minerals, and used them to produce healing drugs. The clock and the calendar we use today are based on Sumerian methods of measuring time.

> Which Sumerian invention greatly improved farm production?
> _____
> _____

THE ARTS OF SUMER

Sumerian remains reveal great skill in **architecture**. A pyramid-shaped **ziggurat** dominated each city. Most people lived in one-story houses with rooms arranged around a small courtyard.

> Underline the sentence that describes the kind of houses in which most Sumerians lived.

Sumerian art is renowned for sculpture and jewelry. Sculptors created statues of gods for the temples, and made small objects of ivory or rare woods. Jewelers worked with imported gold, silver, and fine stones. Earrings and other items found in the region show that Sumerian jewelers knew advanced methods for putting gold pieces together.

The Sumerians also developed a special art form called the cylinder seal. The cylinder seal was a small stone cylinder that was engraved with designs and could be rolled over wet clay to decorate containers or to "sign" documents.

Music played an important role in Sumerian society. Musicians played stringed instruments, reed pipes, drums, and tambourines both for entertainment and for special occasions.

> Name four types of musical instruments played by Sumerians.
> _____
> _____
> _____
> _____

CHALLENGE ACTIVITY

Critical Thinking: Drawing Inferences Consider the invention of writing and of the wheel. As you go through a normal day keep a list of the things you do that rely on one or the other of these two inventions.
HSS Analysis Skills HI 2, HI 3

Mesopotamia and the Fertile Crescent

MAIN IDEAS

1. The Babylonians conquered Mesopotamia and created a code of law.
2. Later invasions of Mesopotamia changed the region's culture.
3. The Phoenicians built a trading society in the eastern Mediterranean region.

 HSS 6.2

Students analyze the geographic, political, economic, religious, and social structures of the early civilizations of Mesopotamia, Egypt, and Kush.

Key Terms and People

monarch a ruler of a kingdom or empire

Hammurabi's Code the earliest known written collection of laws, comprising 282 laws that dealt with almost every part of life

chariot a wheeled, horse-drawn battle car

Nebuchadnezzar the Chaldean king who rebuilt Babylon

alphabet a set of letters than can be combined to form written words

Section Summary

THE BABYLONIANS CONQUER MESOPOTAMIA

By 1800 BC, a powerful city-state had arisen in Babylon, an old Sumerian city on the Euphrates. Babylon's greatest **monarch** (MAH-nark), Hammurabi, conquered all of Mespotamia.

> On what river was the city of Babylon located?
> _____
> _____

During his 42-year reign, Hammurabi oversaw many building and irrigation projects, improved the tax collection system, and brought prosperity through increased trade. He is most famous, however, for **Hammurabi's Code**, the earliest known written collection of laws. It contained laws on everything from trade, loans, and theft to injury, marriage, and murder. Some of its ideas are still found in laws today. The code was important not only for how thorough it was, but also because it was written down for all to see.

> Why do you think it is important for laws to be written down?
> _____
> _____
> _____
> _____

INVASIONS OF MESOPOTAMIA

Several other civilizations developed in and around the Fertile Crescent. As their armies battled each other for Mesopotamia's fertile land, control of the region passed from one empire to another. The Hittites of Asia Minor captured Babylon in 1595 BC with strong iron weapons and the skillful use of the **chariot** on the battlefield. After the Hittite king was killed, the Kassites captured Babylon and ruled for almost 400 years.

The Assyrians were the next group to conquer all of Mesopotamia. They ruled from Nineveh, a city in the north. The Assyrians collected taxes, enforced laws, and raised troops through local leaders. The Assyrians also built roads to link distant parts of the empire. In 612 BC the Chaldeans, a group from the Syrian Desert, conquered the Assyrians.

Nebuchadnezzar (neb-uh-kuhd-NEZ-uhr), the most famous Chaldean king, rebuilt Babylon into a beautiful city. According to legend, his grand palace featured the famous Hanging Gardens. The Chaldeans revived Sumerian culture and made notable advances in astronomy and mathematics.

> **Name four groups that conquered all of Mesopotamia after the Babylonians.**
> _____
> _____
> _____
> _____
> _____

> **Which older Mesopotamian civilization did the Chaldeans admire and study?**
> _____
> _____

THE PHOENICIANS

Phoenicia, at the western end of the Fertile Crescent along the Mediterranean Sea, created a wealthy trading society. Fleets of fast Phoenician trading ships sailed throughout the Mediterrranean and even into the Atlantic Ocean, building trade networks and founding new cities. The Phoenicians' most lasting achievement, however, was the **alphabet**, a major development that has had a huge impact on the ancient world and on our own.

> **On what body of water were most Phoenician colonies located?**
> _____
> _____

CHALLENGE ACTIVITY

Critical Thinking: Drawing Inferences Make a timeline with approximate dates showing the various empires and invasions that characterized the history of Mesopotamia up to the time of the Chaldeans. **HSS Analysis Skills CS 2, HI 1, HI 2**

Ancient Egypt

HISTORY–SOCIAL SCIENCE STANDARDS

HSS 6.2 Students analyze the geographic, political, economic, social, and religious structures of the early civilizations of Mesopotamia, Egypt, and Kush.
HSS Analysis Skill HR 4 Assess the credibility of primary and secondary sources.

CHAPTER SUMMARY

Hunter-Gatherers 9500 BC	First Villages 4500 BC	The First Pharaoh 3100 BC	1570 BC The New Kingdom

COMPREHENSION AND CRITICAL THINKING

Use information from the graphic organizer to answer the following questions.

1. Explain Who were the earliest settlers of the Nile and why did they settle there?

_____

_____

2. Identify Cause and Effect When and why did villages first form in the Nile Valley?

_____

_____

3. Evaluate How did the first pharaoh and his descendents impact Egyptian life?

_____

_____

4. Draw a Conclusion What was the biggest difference between the original Nile settlers and residents of the New Kingdom?

_____

_____

30

Name Galilea Trinidad   Class 44   Date 1-23-16

Ancient Egypt

Section 1

┌─────────────────────────────────────┐
│ **MAIN IDEAS** │
│ 1. Egypt was called "the gift of the Nile" │
│   because the Nile River was so important. │
│ 2. Civilization developed after people began │
│   farming along the Nile. │
│ 3. Strong kings unified all of Egypt. │
└─────────────────────────────────────┘

 HSS 6.2
Students analyze the geographic, political, economic, social, and religious structures of the early civilizations of Mesopotamia, Egypt, and Kush.

Key Terms and People

cataract steep river rapids, almost impossible to sail by boat

delta triangle-shaped area of land made of soil deposited by a river

Menes Egyptian leader who united both upper and lower Egypt into one kingdom

pharaoh ruler of unified Egypt, literally means "great house"

dynasty series of rulers from the same family

Section Summary

THE GIFT OF THE NILE

The existence of Egypt was based solely around the Nile, the world's longest river. The Nile carries water from central Africa through a vast stretch of desert land. The river was so important to people that Egypt was called "the gift of the Nile."

Ancient Egypt developed along a 750-mile stretch of the Nile, and was originally organized into two kingdoms—Upper Egypt and Lower Egypt. Upper Egypt was located upriver in relation to the Nile's flow. Lower Egypt was the northern region and was located downriver.

Cataracts, or steep rapids, marked the southern border of Upper Egypt. Lower Egypt was centered in the river **delta**, a triangle-shaped area of land made of soil deposited by the river. In midsummer, the Nile would flood Upper Egypt and in the fall the river would flood Lower Egypt. This made sure that the farmland would stay moist and fertile. As the

> **Why is a river a "gift" to a desert land?**
>
> The river was so important to people that Egypt was called the gift of the nile

> **How could a cataract serve as a natural protective barrier?**
>
> Cataracts or steep rapids marked the southern border of Upper Egypt.

Interactive Reader and Study Guide

Name Galilea Trinidad   Class 44   Date 1-23-16

Section 1, *continued*

land surrounding the Nile Valley was arid desert, this watered area was the lifeline for everyone who lived in the region.

CIVILIZATION DEVELOPS IN EGYPT

With dry desert all around, it is no wonder that ancient settlers were attracted to this abundant and protected area of fertile farmland. Hunter-gatherers first moved to the area around 12,000 years ago and found plenty of meat and fish to hunt and eat. By 4500 BC farmers were living in villages and growing wheat and barley. They were also raising cattle and sheep.

Around 3200 BC the Egyptian villages became organized into two kingdoms. The capital of Lower Egypt was located in the northwest Nile Delta at a town called Pe. The capital city of Upper Egypt was called Nekhen. It was located on the west bank of the Nile.

> **Why did hunter-gatherers move to the Nile Valley?**
>
> this is abundant and protected area of fertile farmland.

> **Why do you think Egyptian farming villages banded together and became kingdoms?**
>
> Around 3200 BC the Egytian villages became organized into two Kingdoms.

KINGS UNIFY EGYPT

Around 3100 BC **Menes** (MEE-neez), the king of Upper Egypt, invaded Lower Egypt. He married a princess there in order to unite the two kingdoms under his rule. Menes was the first **pharaoh**, which literally means ruler of a "great house." He also started the first Egyptian **dynasty**, or series of rulers from the same family. He built a new capital city, Memphis, which became a popular cultural center. His dynasty ruled for nearly 200 years.

CHALLENGE ACTIVITY

Critical Thinking: Drawing Inferences Villages did not develop until people stopped being hunter-gatherers and started growing their own food. From villages grew powerful leaders who united larger territories and people under one organization. Imagine that you are an ancient Egyptian interested in becoming a leader. Write a speech explaining what would make you a powerful person fit for ruling a large village.

HSS Analysis Skills CS 1, CS 3, HR 3, HR 4, HR 6

Interactive Reader and Study Guide

Ancient Egypt

MAIN IDEAS

1. The Middle Kingdom was a period of stable government between periods of disorder.

2. The New Kingdom was the peak of Egyptian trade and military power, but their greatness did not last.

3. Work and daily life were different among Egypt's social classes.

 HSS 6.2
Students analyze the geographic, political, economic, social, and religious structures of the early civilizations of Mesopotamia, Egypt, and Kush.

Key Terms and People

Middle Kingdom period of stability and order in ancient Egypt between about 2050 and 1750 BC

New Kingdom the height of Egypt's power and glory, between 1550 and 1050 BC

trade routes paths followed by traders

Queen Hatshepsut New Kingdom ruler renowned for expanding Egyptian trade

Ramses the Great important New Kingdom pharaoh who defended Egypt from invaders and strengthened defenses

Section Summary

THE MIDDLE KINGDOM

The Old Kingdom ended with the pharaohs in debt. Ambitious nobles serving in government positions managed to take power from the pharaohs and rule Egypt for nearly 160 years. Finally, a powerful pharaoh regained control of Egypt around 2050 BC and started a peaceful period of rule. This era was called the **Middle Kingdom** and lasted until Southwest Asian invaders conquered Lower Egypt around 1750 BC.

> **From where did the raiders who ended the Middle Kingdom come?**
>
> the _____
>
> _____

THE NEW KINGDOM

When an Egyptian named Ahmose (AHM-ohs) drove away the invaders and declared himself king of Egypt in 1550 BC, he ushered in Egypt's eighteenth dynasty and the start of the **New Kingdom**.

Responding to invasions, Egypt took control of
possible invasion routes and quickly became the
leading military power in the region, with an
empire extending from the Euphrates River in the
northeast to Nubia in the south. These conquests
also made Egypt rich, through gifts and vastly
expanded **trade routes**. One ruler in particular,
Queen Hatshepshut, was active in establishing new
paths for traders.

Despite the strong leadership of **Ramses the
Great**, a tide of invasions from Southwest Asia and
from the west eventually reduced Egypt to violence
and disorder.

> Which direction would you go
> from Egypt to reach Nubia?
> _____
> _____

WORK AND DAILY LIFE

During the Middle and New Kingdoms, Egypt's
population continued to grow and become more
complex. Professional and skilled workers like
scribes, artisans, artists, and architects were
honored. These roles in society were usually passed
on in families, with young boys learning a trade
from their fathers.

> Which professional workers
> probably designed the pyramids?
> _____
> _____

For farmers and peasants, who made up the vast
majority of the population, life never changed.
In addition to hard work on the land, they were
required to pay taxes and were subject to special
labor duty at any time. Only slaves were beneath
them in social status.

> For farmers, did daily life in Egypt
> change much with the rise and fall
> of dynasties and kingdoms?

Most Egyptian families lived in their own homes.
Boys were expected to marry young and start their
own families. Women focused on the home, but
many also had jobs outside the home. Egyptian
women had the legal rights to own property, make
contracts, and divorce their husbands.

CHALLENGE ACTIVITY

Critical Thinking: Drawing Inferences Design an ancient Egyptian "job
want ad," then write a letter to a potential employer explaining why you
should be hired. **HSS Analysis Skills HR 1, HI 6**

Ancient Egypt

Section 4

MAIN IDEAS
1. Egyptian writing used hieroglyphics.
2. Egypt's great temples were lavishly decorated.
3. Egyptian art filled tombs.

 HSS 6.2
Students analyze the geographic, political, economic, social, and religious structures of the early civilizations of Mesopotamia, Egypt, and Kush.

Key Terms and People

hieroglyphics Egyptian writing system, one of the world's first, which used symbols

papyrus long-lasting, paper-like substance made from reeds

Rosetta Stone a stone slab discovered in 1799, that was inscribed with hieroglyphics and their Greek meanings

sphinxes huge ancient Egyptian statues of imaginary creatures with the heads of people and bodies of lions

obelisk a tall, four-sided pillar that is pointed on top

King Tutankhamen pharaoh whose tomb was discovered untouched by raiders, leaving much information about Egyptian art and burial practices

Section Summary

EGYPTIAN WRITING

Egyptians invented one of the world's first writing systems, using a series of images, symbols, and pictures called **hieroglyphics** (hy-ruh-GLIH-fiks). Each symbol represented one or more sounds in the Egyptian language.

At first hieroglyphics were carved in stone. Later, they were written with brushes and ink on **papyrus** (puh-PY-ruhs). Because papyrus didn't decay, many ancient Egyptian texts still survive, including government records, historical records, science texts, medical manuals, and literary works such as *The Book of the Dead*. The discovery of the **Rosetta Stone** in 1799 provided the key to reading Egyptian writing, as its text was inscribed both in hieroglyphics and in Greek.

> **What language helped scholars to understand the meaning of hieroglyphics on the Rosetta Stone?**
>
> _____
>
> _____

EGYPT'S GREAT TEMPLES

Egyptian architects are known not only for the pyramids but also for their magnificent temples. The temples were lavishly designed with numerous statues and beautifully painted walls and pillars. **Sphinxes** and **obelisks** were usually found near the entrances to the temples.

> Besides architects, what two groups of skilled artists worked to decorate Egyptian temples?
>
> _____
>
> _____
>
> _____

EGYPTIAN ART

Ancient Egyptians were masterful artists and many of their greatest works are found in either the temples or the tombs of the pharaohs. Most Egyptians, however, never saw these paintings, because only kings, priests, or other important people could enter these places.

> Who got to see ancient Egyptian sculpture and painting?
>
> _____
>
> _____
>
> _____

Egyptian paintings depict a variety of subjects, from crowning kings to illustrating religious rituals to showing scenes from daily life. The paintings also have a particular style, with people drawn as if they were twisting as they walked, and in different sizes depending upon their stature in society. In contrast, animals appear more realistically. The Egyptians were also skilled stone and metal workers, creating beautiful statues and jewelry.

> Why is King Tutankhamen's tomb so important for the study of Egyptian history?
>
> _____
>
> _____
>
> _____
>
> _____

Much of what we know about Egyptian art and burial practices comes from the tomb of **King Tutankhamen**, one of the few Egyptian tombs that was left untouched by raiders looking for valuables. The tomb was discovered in 1922.

CHALLENGE ACTIVITY

Critical Thinking: Drawing Inferences Using the library or an online resource, find a key to translate Egyptian hieroglyphics into English. Write a message using hieroglyphics and trade off with another student to see if you can read each other's messages. Be sure to provide a copy of your message and the translation to your teacher. **HSS Analysis Skills HR 4, HI 5**

Ancient Kush

HISTORY–SOCIAL SCIENCE STANDARDS
HSS 6.2 Students analyze the geographic, political, economic, religious, and social structures of the early civilizations of Mesopotamia, Egypt, and Kush.
HSS Analysis Skill HI 2 Understand and distinguish cause and effect.

CHAPTER SUMMARY

Egypt	Kush
women worked in the home	women worked in _____
led by pharaohs (male)	led by _____
developed pictograph writing style called _____	developed pictograph writing style called Meroitic
built _____ pyramids to bury dead kings	built _____ pyramids to bury dead kings

COMPREHENSION AND CRITICAL THINKING

Use the answers to the following questions to fill in the graphic organizer above.

1. Explain What were three similarities between the Kush and Egyptian cultures.

_____

2. Identify Cause and Effect How was the position of women in Kush society different than that of Egyptian women?

_____

3. Evaluate Why do you think people's houses were different in Kush and Egypt?

_____

4. Draw a Conclusion How similar are the two cultures? How distinctly different?

_____

_____

Ancient Kush

MAIN IDEAS

1. Geography helped the early Kush civilization develop in Nubia.

2. Egypt controlled Kush for about 500 years.

3. Kush ruled Egypt after winning its independence and set up a new dynasty there.

 HSS 6.2

Students analyze the geographic, political, economic, religious, and social structures of the early civilizations of Mesopotamia, Egypt, and Kush.

Key Terms and People

ebony a type of dark, heavy wood

ivory a white material made from elephant tusks

Piankhi Kushite king who conquered all of Egypt

Section Summary

GEOGRAPHY AND EARLY KUSH

The kingdom of Kush developed south of Egypt along the Nile, in the region we now call Nubia. Every year, floods provided a rich layer of fertile soil. Farming villages thrived. The area was also rich in minerals such as gold, copper, and stone. These resources contributed to the region's wealth.

> What valuable minerals were important to Kush's prosperity?
>
> _____
> _____
> _____

Over time some rich farmers became leaders of their villages. Around 2000 BC, one of these leaders took control of other villages and made himself king of Kush.

> Around what year did the first king of Kush appear?
>
> _____
> _____

The kings of Kush ruled from their capital at Kerma (KAR-muh). The city was located on the Nile just south of a cataract, or stretch of shallow rapids. Because the Nile's cataracts made parts of the river hard to pass through, they were natural barriers against invaders.

As time passed Kushite society became more complex. In addition to farmers and herders, some people of Kush became priests and artisans.

Name _____ Class _____ Date _____

Section 1, *continued*

EGYPT CONTROLS KUSH

Kush and Egypt were neighbors and trading
partners. The Kushites sent slaves to Egypt. They
also sent gold, copper, and stone, as well as the
prized materials **ebony** and **ivory**.

Relations between Kush and Egypt were not
always peaceful, however. Around 1500 BC Egyptian
armies under the pharaoh Thutmose I invaded and
conquered most of Nubia, including all of Kush.
The Kushite palace at Kerma was destroyed. Kush
remained an Egyptian territory until about
1050 BC, when the Kushites rose up and won their
independence.

> For about how many years was
> Kush under Egyptian control?
> _____
> _____

KUSH RULES EGYPT

By around 850 BC, Kush was once again as strong
as it had been before it had been conquered by
Egypt. During the 700s, under the king Kashta,
the Kushites began to invade Egypt. Kashta's son,
Piankhi (PYANG-kee), believed that the gods
wanted him to rule all of Egypt. By the time he died
in 716 BC, Piankhi had accomplished this task. His
kingdom extended from the new Kushite capital,
Napata, all the way to the Nile Delta.

Piankhi's brother, Shabaka (SHAB-uh-kuh),
declared himself pharaoh and began the
twenty-fifth dynasty, or Kushite dynasty, in Egypt.
Egyptian culture thrived during the twenty-fifth
dynasty. About 670 BC, however, the powerful army
of the Assyrians from Mesopotamia invaded Egypt.
The Assyrians' iron weapons were better than the
Kushites' bronze weapons. The Kushites were slowly
pushed back to Nubia.

> Powerful rulers sometimes say
> that God or "the gods" want them
> to expand their power. Do you
> think this is really true? Name
> another motive such leaders might
> have.
> _____
> _____

> The Assyrians' weapons were
> made of what metal?
>
> The Kushites' weapons were made
> of what metal?
> _____
> _____

CHALLENGE ACTIVITY

Critical Thinking: Making Judgments Some leaders do not take control
of other lands and people, even though they have the power to do so.
What does this tell you about village leaders who make themselves kings
over whole regions? **HSS Analysis Skills HR 2, HR 4, HR 5, HI 2**

Interactive Reader and Study Guide

Ancient Kush

MAIN IDEAS

1. Kush's economy grew because if its iron industry and its trade network.

2. Society and culture had elements borrowed from other cultures and elements unique to Kush.

3. The decline and defeat of Kush was caused by both internal and external factors.

 HSS 6.2
Students analyze the geographic, political, economic, religious, and social structures of the early civilizations of Mesopotamia, Egypt, and Kush.

Key Terms and People

trade network a system of people in different lands who trade goods back and forth

merchants traders

exports items sent for sale in other countries or regions

imports goods brought in from other countries or regions

Queen Shanakhdakheto the first woman to rule Kush

King Ezana Aksumite king who destroyed Meroë and took over the kingdom of Kush

Section Summary

KUSH'S ECONOMY GROWS

After they lost control of Egypt and were pushed back to Nubia, the people of Kush devoted themselves to increasing agriculture and trade, hoping to make their country rich again. The economic center of Kush during this period was Meroë (MER-oh-wee). Large deposits of gold could be found nearby, as could forests of ebony and other wood. In this rich location the Kushites developed Africa's first iron industry. Iron ore and wood for furnaces were easily available, so the iron industry grew quickly.

In time, Meroë became the center of a large **trade network**. The Kushites sent goods down the Nile to Egypt. From there, Egyptian and Greek **merchants** shipped goods to ports on the Mediterranean and Red seas, and to southern Africa. These goods may

By what name do we know the Kushite homeland?

_____

_____

What industry helped make Kush a rich and successful kingdom again?

_____

_____

have eventually reached India and perhaps China.
Kush's **exports** included gold, pottery, iron tools,
ivory, leopard skins, ostrich feathers, elephants,
and slaves. **Imports** included fine jewelry and
luxury items from Egypt, Asia, and lands along the
Mediterranean.

SOCIETY AND CULTURE

The most obvious influence on Kush during this
period was Egyptian, but many elements of Kushite
culture were not borrowed from anywhere else.
The people of Kush worshipped their own gods and
even developed their own written language. Women
were expected to be active in their society. Some
women rose to positions of great authority, especially
in religion. **Queen Shanakhdakheto** was (shah-
nahk-dah-KEE-toh) the first of several queens who
ruled the empire alone, helping to increase Kush's
strength and wealth.

> How was the position of women
> in Kushite society different than
> that of women in most other
> ancient civilizations?
> _____
> _____
> _____
> _____

DECLINE AND DEFEAT

Kushite civilization reached its height in the first
century BC. Eventually it fell due to both external
and internal factors. The stores of iron and other
metals dwindled, and the overgrazing of cattle
caused a deterioration of farmland. Another
powerful trading center, Aksum (AHK-soom),
located in modern-day Eritrea, began competing
with Kush. Soon trade routes were bypassing
Meroë for Aksum. After Aksum had decimated
Kush economically, the Aksumite leader **King Ezana**
(AY-zah-nah) sent an invading army and conquered
the once-powerful Kush.

> Circle the name and kingdom of
> the ruler who eventually defeated
> Kush.

CHALLENGE ACTIVITY

Critical Thinking: Drawing Inferences You are a Kushite leader in 50
BC. Write a short essay explaining your plan to build up Kush's strength
and make it possible to defeat Egypt. **HSS Analysis Skills HR 1, HR 4,
HI 1, HI 4, HI 5**

Name _____ Class _____ Date _____

Ancient India

HISTORY–SOCIAL SCIENCE STANDARDS
HSS 6.5 Students analyze the geographic, political, economic, religious, and social structures of the early civilizations of India.

CHAPTER SUMMARY

Aryan invasion of Indus and Ganges	led to	**development of the caste system**
unification of India into empires	led to	**stability and prosperity**
development of religion	led to	**changes in roles of early Indian kings**
stability of early Indian empires	led to	**advances in arts and sciences**

COMPREHENSION AND CRITICAL THINKING

Use information from the graphic organizer to answer the following questions.

1. Recall Which group introduced and developed the caste system in India?

_____

_____

2. Identify Cause and Effect Why does the unification of civilizations usually lead to prosperity and stability?

_____

_____

3. Evaluate Why do you think religion played such an important role in the way rulers were regarded in early civilizations?

_____

_____

4. Draw a Conclusion What characteristic of a civilization usually provides a sound basis for advances in arts and sciences?

_____

_____

Interactive Reader and Study Guide

Name _GlileaTrinidad_   Class _44_   Date _3-22-17_

Ancient India

Section 1

MAIN IDEAS

1. The geography of India includes high mountains, great rivers and heavy seasonal rain.
2. Harappan civilization developed along the Indus River.
3. The Aryan invasion of India changed the region's civilization.

 HSS 6.5.2
Discuss the significance of the Aryan invasion.

Key Terms and People

subcontinent a large landmass smaller than a continent
monsoon seasonal wind patterns that cause wet and dry seasons
Sanskrit ancient India's most influential language

Section Summary

GEOGRAPHY OF INDIA

India is home to one of the world's earliest civilizations. India is so huge it's called a **subcontinent**, which is a large landmass that is smaller than a continent. A subcontinent is usually separated from a continent by physical features, such as mountains. The world's highest mountains, the Himalayas, are in India. India also has a vast desert, many fertile plains, and rugged plateaus. The Indus River, which flows from the Himalayas and is located mainly in present-day Pakistan, is the cradle of ancient Indian civilization. As in Egypt and Kush, the flooding river created fertile plains where people first settled. India's hot and humid climate is heavily influenced by **monsoons**, wind patterns that cause wet and dry seasons.

> Circle the name of the world's highest mountains.

> What two natural cycles affected agricultural development in the Indus valley?
> _____
> _____
> _____

HARAPPAN CIVILIZATION

India's first civilization was the Harappan civilization, which developed along the Indus River valley. Named after the ancient city of Harappa, archaeologists believe Harappans thrived between 2300 and 1700 BC. In fact, most information about Harappans comes from the ruins of Harappa and another major city, Mohenjo Daro. Each city was well planned and built in the shadow of a fortress that could easily oversee the city streets.

The cities were very advanced. Most houses had indoor plumbing. The Harappans developed beautiful artisan crafts and a system of weights and measures. They also developed India's first writing system, but scholars have not been able to read it. Because of this, we know little for sure about the Harappan government, though it is thought that there were kings, who might have been thought of as gods. It's also unclear why the Harappan civilization crumbled.

> **Why was it an advantage for the streets of Mohenjo Daro and Harappa to be viewed from a fortress?**
> _____
> _____
> _____
> _____

> **Why do we know so little about the Harappans?**
> _____
> _____
> _____

ARYAN INVASION

Originally nomads from Central Asia, the Aryans had taken over the Indus and Ganges River valleys by 1200 BC. Unlike the Harappans, they had no central government and they did not build planned cities. Aryans lived in small communities run by a local leader, or raja. Aryan groups fought each other as often as they fought outsiders.

The Aryans spoke **Sanskrit** and developed a rich tradition of sacred texts that survived from generation to generation by word of mouth. People later figured out how to write in Sanskrit. The huge lasting influence of these early written works made Sanskrit the most important language of ancient India. Much of what we know about the early Aryans comes to us through Sanskrit records.

> **The early Aryans had a rich and expressive language, but they did not write. How did they preserve their sacred texts without writing?**
> _____
> _____
> _____
> _____

CHALLENGE ACTIVITY

Critical Thinking: Drawing Inferences Write a short essay explaining what you think might have happened to the Harappan civilization.
HSS Analysis Skills CR 1, CR 3, HI 4, HI 5

Interactive Reader and Study Guide

Ancient India

MAIN IDEAS

1. Indian society divided into distinct social classes under the Aryans.
2. The Aryans practiced a religion known as Brahmanism.
3. Hinduism developed out of Brahmanism and influences from other cultures.
4. The Jains reacted to Hinduism by breaking away to form their own religion.

 HSS 6.5.3
Explain the major beliefs and practices of Brahmanism in India and how they evolved into early Hinduism.

Key Terms and People

caste system a division of Indian society into groups based on a person's birth, wealth, or occupation

Hinduism the most widespread religion in India today

reincarnation the belief that the soul, once a person dies, is reborn in another person

karma the effects that good or bad actions have on a person's soul

Jainism a nonviolent religion based on the teachings of Mahavira

nonviolence the avoidance of violent actions

Section Summary

INDIAN SOCIETY DIVIDES

Aryan society was divided into social classes. There were four main groups, called *varnas*. The Brahmins (BRAH-muhns) were priests and were the highest ranking varna. The Kshatriyas (KSHA-tree-uhs) were rulers or warriors. The Vaisyas (VYSH-yuhs) were commoners, including farmers, craftspeople, and traders. The Sudras (SOO-drahs) were laborers and servants.

This **caste system** became more complex, dividing Indian society into groups based on rank, wealth or occupation. Castes were family based. If you were born into a caste, you would probably stay in it for your whole life. Life for the lower castes was difficult, but those who had no caste, called untouchables, were ostracized.

> Rank the main groups of the Aryan social classes in order of importance, with one (1) being highest and four (4) being the lowest:
> Brahmins
> Sudras
> Kshatriyas
> Vaisyas

> In ancient India, why was it important to belong to some caste?
> _____
> _____
> _____

BRAHMANISM

The religion practiced by the Brahmins became
known as Brahmanism. Brahmanism was perhaps
the most important part of ancient Indian life, as
shown by the high status of the priest caste. The
religion was based on the four Vedas, sacred texts
that contained ancient sacred hymns and poems.
Over time, Aryan Brahmins and scholars wrote
their thoughts about the Vedas. These thoughts
were compiled into Vedic texts. The texts described
rituals, explained how to perform sacrifices, and
offered reflections from religious scholars.

> **What do the Vedic texts describe?**
> _____
> _____
> _____

HINDUISM DEVELOPS

Hinduism is India's largest religion today. It
developed from Brahmanism and other influences.
Hindus believe that there are many deities, but all
deities are part of a universal spirit called Brahmin.
Hindus believe everyone has a soul, or atman, and
the soul longs to join with Brahmin. This happens
when the soul recognizes that the world we live in is
an illusion. Hindus believe this understanding takes
several lifetimes, so **reincarnation**, or rebirth, is
necessary. How you are reborn depends upon your
karma, or your actions in life. In the caste system,
those who have good karma are born to higher
castes. Those with bad karma are born into lower
castes or maybe even an animal.

> **What is the Hindu name for the soul?**
> _____
> _____

> **What is karma?**
> _____
> _____

The religion of **Jainism** developed in reaction to
Hinduism. Jainism is based upon the principle of
nonviolence, or ahimsa.

CHALLENGE ACTIVITY

Critical Thinking: Drawing Inferences Do ahimsa, reincarnation, or
karma have any relevance in our society? Pick one or more of these
terms and write a one-page essay on how such terms could, or could
not, be used in your world. **HSS Analysis Skills CR 5, HI 3**

Ancient India

MAIN IDEAS

1. Siddhartha Gautama searched for wisdom in many ways.
2. The teachings of Buddhism deal with finding peace.
3. Buddhism spread far from where it began in India.

 HSS 6.5.5

Know the life and moral teachings of the Buddha and how Buddhism spread in India, Ceylon, and Central Asia.

Key Terms and People

fasting going without food

meditation focusing the mind on spiritual ideas

the Buddha the "Enlightened One"

Buddhism religion based on the teachings of the Buddha

nirvana a state of perfect peace

missionaries people who spread and teach religious beliefs

Section Summary

SIDDARTHA'S SEARCH FOR WISDOM

Not everyone in India accepted Hinduism. In the late 500s BC, a major new religion began to develop from questions posed by a young prince named Siddhartha Gautama (si-DAHR-tuh GAU-tuh-muh). Siddhartha was born to a wealthy family and led a life of comfort, but he wondered at the pain and suffering he saw all around him. By the age of 30, Siddharta left his home and family to travel India. He talked to many priests and wise men, but he was not satisfied with their answers.

Siddhartha did not give up. He wandered for years through the forests trying to free himself from daily concerns by **fasting** and **meditating**. After six years, Siddhartha sat down under a tree and meditated for seven weeks. He came up with an answer to what causes human suffering. Suffering is caused by wanting what one does not have, wanting

> **Why did Prince Siddhartha leave a comfortable home and loving family?**
> _____
> _____
> _____

> **Can you think of a form of human suffering not covered by one of Siddhartha's three categories? If so, state briefly what it is.**
> _____
> _____
> _____
> _____

to keep what one likes and already has, and not wanting what one dislikes but has. He began to travel and teach his ideas, and was soon called **the Buddha**, or "Enlightened One." From his teachings sprang the religion **Buddhism**.

TEACHINGS OF BUDDHISM

Buddhism is intent on relieving human suffering. It is based upon the Four Noble Truths. These truths are: Suffering and unhappiness are part of life; suffering stems from our desire for pleasure and material goods; people can overcome their desires and reach **nirvana**, a state of perfect peace, which ends the cycle of reincarnation; and people can follow an eightfold path to nirvana, overcoming desire and ignorance.

> **What is the name of the central teachings of Buddhism?**
> _____
> _____

These teachings were similar to some Hindu concepts, but went against some traditional Hindu ideas. Buddhism questioned the need for animal sacrifice. It also challenged the authority of the Brahmins. The Buddha said that each individual could reach salvation on his or her own. Buddhism also opposed the caste system.

> **Buddhist texts often refer to "the compassionate Buddha." Why is this term appropriate?**
> _____
> _____
> _____

BUDDHISM SPREADS

Buddhism spread quickly throughout India. With the help of Indian king Asoka, Buddhist **missionaries** were sent to other countries to teach their religious beliefs. Buddhism quickly took hold in neighboring countries like Nepal, Sri Lanka, and China. Buddhism soon became very influential in Japan and Korea. In modern times, Buddhism has become a major global religion.

> **Where did Buddhism spread?**
> _____
> _____
> _____

CHALLENGE ACTIVITY

Critical Thinking: Drawing Inferences Could you leave your family, home, and everything you know to preach what you believe to be a spiritual truth? Write a dialogue between a young person preparing to follow the Buddha and his or her family. Explain why he or she has chosen this life of sacrifice. **HSS Analysis Skills CR 2, CR 4, HI 3**

Ancient India

MAIN IDEAS

1. The Mauryan Empire unified most of India.
2. Gupta rulers promoted Hinduism within their empires.

 HSS 6.1
Describe the growth of the Maurya Empire and the political and moral achievements of the emperor Asoka.

Key Terms and People

Chandragupta Maurya Indian military leader who first unified India and founded the Mauryan Empire

Asoka Chandragupta's grandson and last ruler of the Mauryan Empire

Chandragupta II ruler who brought great prosperity and stability to India

Academic Vocabulary

establish to set up or create

Section Summary

MAURYAN EMPIRE UNIFIES INDIA

Under Aryan rule, India was divided into several states with no central leader. Then, during the 300s BC, the conquests of Alexander the Great brought much of India into his empire. An Indian military leader named **Chandragupta Maurya** followed Alexander's example and seized control of the entire northern part of India. The Mauryan Empire lasted for 150 years.

> Who inspired Indian leader Chandragupta Maurya to unify India for the first time?
> _____
> _____

Chandragupta's complex government included a huge army and a network of spies. He taxed the population heavily for the protection he offered. Eventually, Chandragupta became a Jainist monk and gave up his throne to his son. His family continued to expand the Indian empire.

Chandragupta's grandson, **Asoka**, was the strongest ruler of the Mauryan dynasty. The empire thrived under his rule. But at last, tired of killing and war, Asoka converted to Buddhism. He sent Buddhist missionaries to other countries and

> What is the relationship between Chandragupta's government and the heavy taxes?
> _____
> _____
> _____
> _____
> _____

devoted the rest of his rule to improving the lives of his people. The rest of the family, however, did not follow Asoka's example. When Asoka died, his sons struggled for power and foreign invaders threatened the country. The Mauryan Empire fell in 184 BC India remained divided for about 500 years. The spread of Buddhism steadily increased, while Hinduism declined.

> Asoka is sometimes regarded as proof that national security can coexist with peace. Do you think a leader like Asoka could be effective in the world today? Why or why not?

GUPTA RULERS PROMOTE HINDUISM

A new dynasty was **established** in India. During the AD 300s, the Gupta Dynasty once again rose to unite and build the prosperity of India. Not only did the Guptas control India's military, they were devout Hindus and encouraged the revival of Hindu traditions and writings. The Guptas, however, also supported Jainism and Buddhism.

> Which dynasty again united India and revived Hindu traditions?

Indian civilization reached a high point under **Chandragupta II** (not related to Chandragupta Maurya). He poured money and resources into strengthening the country's borders, as well as promoting the arts, literature, and religion.

The Guptas believed the caste system supported stability. This was not good for women, whose role under the empire was very restricted. Women were expected to marry, in weddings arranged by their parents, and raise children. A woman had to obey her husband and had few rights.

> Name two flaws, from a democratic point of view, in Indian civilization under the Guptas.

The Gupta Dynasty lasted until fierce attacks by the Huns from Central Asia during the 400s drained the empire of its resources. India broke up once again into a patchwork of small states.

CHALLENGE ACTIVITY

Critical Thinking: Drawing Inferences Asoka was strongly influenced by Buddhism. Chandragupta II followed Hinduism. Write an essay explaining which king you think was a better leader. How did their religion affect their rule? Keep in mind the situation of Indian society under both kings' reign. **HSS Analysis Skills CS 1, CR 5, HI 6**

Ancient India

MAIN IDEAS

1. Indian artists created great works of religious art.
2. Sanskrit literature flourished during the Gupta period.
3. The Indians made scientific advances in metalworking, medicine and other sciences.

 HSS 6.5

Discuss important aesthetic and intellectual traditions (e.g., Sanskrit literature, including the Bhagavad Gita; medicine; metallurgy; and mathematics, including Hindu-Arabic numerals and the zero.

Key Terms and People

metallurgy the science of working with metals

alloy a mixture of two or more metals

Hindu-Arabic numerals the numbering system invented by Indian mathematicians and brought to Europe by Arabs; the numbers we use today

inoculation a method of injecting a person with a small dose of a virus to help him or her build up defenses to a disease

astronomy the study of stars and planets

Academic Vocabulary

process a series of steps by which a task is completed

Section Summary

RELIGIOUS ART

Both the Mauryan and Guptan empires unified India and created a stable environment where artists, writers, scholars, and scientists could thrive. Their works are still admired today. Much of the Indian art from this period was religious, inspired by both Hindu and Buddhist teachings. Many beautiful temples were built during this time and decorated with elaborate wood and stone carvings.

> What was the main inspiration for art and literature during the Mauryan and Guptan empires?
> _____
> _____

SANSKRIT LITERATURE

Great works of literature were written in Sanskrit, the ancient Aryan language, during the Gupta

Name _____ Class _____ Date _____

Section 5, *continued*

Dynasty. The best-known works are sacred texts
called the *Mahabharata* (muh-HAH-BAH-ruh-tuh)
and the *Ramayana* (rah-MAH-yuh-nuh). The
Mahabharata, a long text about the struggle
between good and evil, is considered a classic
Hindu text. The most famous passage is called
the *Bhagavad Gita* (BUG-uh-vuhd-GEE-tah). The
Ramayana tells of the Prince Rama, a human incar-
nation of Vishnu, a Hindu deity, who fights demons
and marries the beautiful princess Sita.

> **What are the *Mahabharata* and the *Ramayana*?**
> _____
> _____
> _____
> _____

SCIENTIFIC ADVANCES

Scientific and scholarly work also blossomed during
the early Indian empires. Most prominent was the
development of **metallurgy**, the science of working
with metals. Indian technicians and engineers made
strong tools and weapons. They also invented
processes for creating **alloys**. Alloys, such as steel or
bronze, may be stronger or more useful than pure
metals like iron or copper.

> **What is the science of working with metals called?**
> _____
> _____

The numbers we use today, called **Hindu-
Arabic numerals**, were first developed by Indian
mathematicians. They also created the concept of
zero, upon which all modern math is based.

> **What mathematical concept expresses the idea of "none"?**
> _____
> _____

Other sciences also benefited from this period
of Indian history. In medicine, Indians developed
the technique of **inoculation**, which is injecting a
person with a small dose of a virus to help him or
her build up defenses to a disease. Doctors could
even perform certain surgeries. India's fascination
with **astronomy**, the study of stars and planets, led
to the discovery of seven of the planets in our solar
system.

> **Indians at this period did not have telescopes. How do you think they discovered planets?**
> _____
> _____
> _____
> _____

CHALLENGE ACTIVITY

Critical Thinking: Drawing Inferences Our modern society borrows
significantly from the scientific and mathematical achievements of the
early Indian empires. Write a short play, story, or essay describing how
our modern world might look without these inventions. **HSS Analysis
Skills CS 1, HI 3.**

Interactive Reader and Study Guide

Name _____ Class _____ Date _____

Ancient China

HISTORY–SOCIAL SCIENCE STANDARDS
HSS 6.6 Students analyze the geographic, political, economic, religious, and social structures of the early civilizations of China.

CHAPTER SUMMARY

THE FIRST FIVE DYNASTIES

XIA 2200 BC: According to legend, the first waterways were built	**SHANG 1500 BC:** Writing system begins	**ZHOU 1100 BC:** Social hierarchy, family structure, central authority	**QIN 220 BC:** Military regime, strong central government, harsh policies, roads, canals, Great Wall	**HAN 200 BC:** Poetry, central government preserved, punishments less severe, paper, acupuncture, trade

COMPREHENSION AND CRITICAL THINKING

Use information from the graphic organizer to answer the following questions.

1. Identify Which of the first five dynasties lasted the longest?

_____

_____

2. Draw Inferences Which dynasty improved on a rudimentary system of communication that had probably existed for 2000 years?

_____

_____

3. Evaluate Which dynasty kept some beneficial aspects of the former regime and ended its harsher aspects?

_____

_____

Interactive Reader and Study Guide

Ancient China

MAIN IDEAS

1. China's physical geography made farming possible but travel and communication difficult.

2. Civilization began in China along the Huang He and Chang Jiang rivers.

3. China's first dynasties helped Chinese society develop and made many other achievements.

 HSS 6.6
Students analyze the geographic, political, economic, religious, and social structures of the early civilizations of China.

Key Terms and People

jade a hard gemstone
oracle a prediction

Section Summary

CHINA'S PHYSICAL GEOGRAPHY

China is a large country with many different geographical features. China is about the same size as the United States. Some geographical features separated groups of people within China, while other features separated China from the rest of the world. These features include the Gobi Desert, which spreads over much of China's north, and rugged mountains on the western frontier.

> In which part of China is the Gobi Desert?
> _____
> _____

Low-lying plains in the east form one of the world's largest farming regions. Weather patterns vary widely across China. Two great rivers flow from west to east, the Huang He, or Yellow River, and the Chang Jiang, or Yangzi River.

CIVILIZATION BEGINS

Like other ancient peoples, people in China first settled along rivers. By 7000 BC farmers grew rice in the Chang Jiang Valley. Along the Huang He, they grew millet and wheat. Early Chinese also fished and hunted with bows and arrows. They raised

> Where did the Chinese first grow rice?
> _____
> _____

pigs and sheep. Separate cultures developed along the two rivers. As populations grew, villages spread. A social order developed. The graves of the rich often contained objects made from **jade**.

CHINA'S FIRST DYNASTIES

Societies along the Huang He grew larger and more complex. Around 2200 BC, a legendary emperor called Yu the Great is said to have founded the Xia (SHAH) dynasty. It is believed that the first flood control channels were built during the Xia dynasty.

> **About how many years ago were the first flood control channels built in China?**
> _____
> _____

The first dynasty for which we have clear evidence is the Shang. It was firmly established by the 1500s BC. The Shang king and his family were at the top of the social order. Nobles and warrior leaders also had high rank. Artisans lived in groups depending on what they did for a living. Farmers worked hard but had little wealth. Taxes claimed much of what they earned. Slaves provided an important source of labor.

The Shang made many advances, including China's first writing system. The Chinese symbols that are used today are based on those of the Shang period. Priests carved questions about the future on cattle bones and turtle shells, which were then heated, causing them to crack. The priests believed they could "read" these cracks to predict the future. For this reason the bones were called **oracle** bones.

> **Which dynasty provided the basis for China's writing system?**
> _____
> _____

Artisans made beautiful bronze containers for cooking and religious ceremonies. They also made ornaments, knives, and axes from jade. The army developed war chariots and bronze body armor. Shang astrologers developed a calendar based on the cycles of the moon.

CHALLENGE ACTIVITY

Critical Thinking: Drawing Inferences Using the library or online resource, study ancient Chinese writing. Use some of these symbols to illustrate something you have learned about China. **HSS Analysis Skills HI 3, HI 4**

Ancient China

MAIN IDEAS

1. The Zhou dynasty expanded China but then declined.
2. Confucius offered ideas to bring order to Chinese society.
3. Daoism and Legalism also gained followers.

 HSS 6.6
Students analyze the geographic, political, economic, religious, and social structures of the early civilizations of China.

Key Terms and People

lords people of high rank

peasants farmers with small farms

Confucius most influential teacher in Chinese history

ethics moral values

Confucianism the ideas of Confucius

Daoism an early Chinese belief that stressed living in harmony with the universe

Laozi the most famous Daoist teacher

Legalism an early Chinese belief that people were bad by nature and needed to be controlled

Academic Vocabulary

structure the way something is set up or organized

Section Summary

THE ZHOU DYNASTY

The Zhou (JOH) came from the west and overthrew the Shang dynasty during the 1100s BC. Their armies defeated people in every direction. They expanded their rule south to the Chang Jiang river. The Zhou established a new political order. The king granted land to **lords** in return for loyalty and military assistance. Lords divided their land among lesser nobles. **Peasants** received a small plot of land and had to farm additional land for a noble. The social order brought by the Zhou lasted a long time, but the loyalty of the lords gradually lessened. They

How did the Zhou establish their rule throughout China?

_____

_____

Interactive Reader and Study Guide

began to fight each other. Family **structure**, which had been the foundation of Chinese life for centuries, was severely weakened. By the 400s BC, China had entered an era called the Warring States period.

CONFUCIUS AND SOCIETY

Toward the end of the Zhou period, a teacher named **Confucius** traveled through China. He taught that order in society stems from **ethics**, or moral values, and not laws. He wanted China to return to the ideas and practices from a time when people knew their proper roles in society. **Confucianism** has been a guiding force in human behavior and religious understanding in China and elsewhere through the centuries.

> Do you think that Confucius's ideas about virtue and kindness are strongly held in American society today? Why or why not?
>
> _____
> _____
> _____
> _____

DAOISM AND LEGALISM

Around the same time as Confucius, other influential beliefs arose in China. **Daoism** (DOW-ih-zum) stressed living in harmony with the Dao, the guiding force of all reality. Daoists believed that people should be like water and simply let things flow in a natural way. They regarded humans as just a part of nature, not superior to any other thing. **Laozi** was the most famous Daoist teacher.

> Underline the sentence that describes the way Daoists regard human life.

   Legalism is different than both Daoism and Confucianism. Legalists believed that society needed strict laws to keep people in line. They believed in unity, efficiency, and punishment for bad conduct. They wanted the empire to continue to expand, so they urged the state to be always prepared for war. Legalists were the first to put their ideas into practice throughout China.

CHALLENGE ACTIVITY

Critical Thinking: Drawing Inferences Write a short play with two characters, a Daoist and a Legalist. Make sure each character clearly expresses his or her views on behavior, society, and government. **HSS Analysis Skills HR 1, HI 1**

Ancient China

MAIN IDEAS

1. The first Qin emperor created a strong but strict government.
2. A unified China was created through Qin policies and achievements.

 HSS 6.6
Students analyze the geographic, political, economic, religious, and social structures of the early civilizations of China.

Key Terms and People

Shi Huangdi literally "first emperor," the title the Qin king Ying Zheng gave himself

Great Wall a barrier built by the Qin that linked earlier walls across China's northern frontier

Section Summary

THE QIN EMPEROR'S STRONG GOVERNMENT

The Warring States period marked a time in China when several states battled each other for power. One state, the Qin (CHIN), built a strong army that defeated the armies of the other states. In 221 BC the Qin king Ying Zheng was able to unify China. He gave himself the title **Shi Huangdi** (SHEE hwahng-dee), which means "first emperor."

Shi Huangdi was a follower of Legalist beliefs. He created a strong government with strict laws and severe punishments. He ordered the burning of all books that did not agree with Legalism.

Shi Huangdi took land away from the lords. He divided China into 36 miltary districts. He made commoners work on goverment building projects.

> **How did Shi Huangdi's rule demonstrate his Legalist beliefs?**
> _____
> _____
> _____
> _____

A UNIFIED CHINA

Qin rule brought other major changes to China. Under Shi Huangdi, new policies and achievements united the Chinese people. The emperor set up a uniform system of law. Rules and punishments were to be the same in all parts of the empire. He also

> **List three ways Shi Huangdi unified China.**
> _____
> _____
> _____
> _____

standardized the written language. People everywhere were required to write using the same set of symbols. People from different regions could now communicate with each other in writing. This gave them a sense of shared culture and a common identity.

Shi Huangdi also set up a new monetary system. Standardized gold and copper coins became the currency for all of China. Weights and measures were also standardized. With all these changes and the unified writing system, trade became much easier. A new network of highways connected the capital to every part of the empire. Workers built canals to connect the country's rivers. Parts of the Qin irrigation system are still used today.

> **Give three reasons why trade flourished under the Qin.**
>
> _____
>
> _____
>
> _____
>
> _____

The completion of the **Great Wall** was a major Qin achievement. The Qin connected earlier pieces of the wall to form a long, unbroken structure that protected China from fierce northern nomads. Building the wall required years of labor from hundreds of thousands of soldiers and workers. Many of them died building the wall.

> **What was the purpose of the Great Wall?**
>
> _____
>
> _____
>
> _____

Although he unified China, many Chinese people hated Shi Huangdi's harsh ways. When he died in 210 BC, rebel forces formed across the country and tried to take over the government. After a period of disorder, the Qin palace was attacked and burned to the ground. Qin authority had disappeared. China fell into civil war.

CHALLENGE ACTIVITY

Critical Thinking: Drawing Inferences If you lived in China and a brutal dictator came to power, would you join a revolutionary group planning to overthrow the government? Be sure to consider the ideas of Confucianism and Daoism in your answer. **HSS Analysis Skills CS 1, HR 1, HR 5, HI 2**

Ancient China

MAIN IDEAS

1. Han dynasty government was based on the ideas of Confucius.

2. Family life strengthened Han China.

3. The Han made many achievements in art, literature, and learning.

 HSS 6.6
Students analyze the geographic, political, economic, religious, and social structures of the early civilizations of China.

Key Terms and People

sundial a device that uses the position of shadows cast by the sun to tell time

seismograph a device that measures the strength of an earthquake

acupuncture the practice of inserting small needles through the skin at specific points to cure disease or relieve pain

Academic Vocabulary

innovation a new idea, method, or device

Section Summary

HAN DYNASTY GOVERNMENT

Liu Bang (lee-oo bang), a peasant, led the army that won control of China after the collapse of the Qin dynasty. He earned the people's loyalty and trust. He lowered taxes for farmers and made punishments less severe. He set up a government that built on the foundation begun by the Qin. Liu Bang's successor, Wudi (woo-dee), made Confucianism the official government policy of China. To get a government job, a person had to pass a test based on Confucian teachings. However, wealthy and influential families still controlled the government.

> **Which feature of the Qin dynasty did the Han preserve?**
> _____
> _____

FAMILY LIFE

A firm social order took hold during Han rule. In the Confucian view, peasants made up the second-highest class. Merchants occupied the lowest class because they merely bought and sold what others

> **Why does Confucian thinking devalue merchants?**
> _____
> _____
> _____

had made. However, this social division did not indicate wealth or power. Peasants were still poor and merchants were still rich.

During Wudi's reign, the family once again became the center of Chinese society. Children were taught from birth to respect their elders. Within the family, the father had absolute power. Han officials believed that if the family was strong and people obeyed the father, then people would obey the emperor, too. Chinese parents valued boys more highly than girls. Some women, however, still gained power. They could influence their sons' families. An older widow could even become the head of the family.

> **Who had absolute power in the family under the Han?**
> _____
> _____

> **Circle the sentence that explains which women could become heads of families.**

HAN ACHIEVEMENTS

The Han dynasty was a time of great accomplishments. Art and literature thrived, and inventors developed many useful devices. Han artists painted portraits and realistic scenes that showed everyday life. Poets developed new styles of verse. Historian Sima Qian wrote a complete history of China until the Han dynasty.

The Han Chinese invented paper. They made it by grinding plant fibers into a paste and then letting it dry in sheets. They made "books" by pasting sheets together into a long sheet that was rolled into a scroll.

> **Name the greatest and most far-reaching Han invention.**
> _____
> _____

Other Han **innovations** included the **sundial** and the **seismograph**. They developed the disinctive Chinese medical practice of **acupuncture** (AK-yoo-punk-cher). These and other Han inventions and advances are still used today.

CHALLENGE ACTIVITY

Critical Thinking: Drawing Inferences Could the Han dynasty have flourished so well if the Qin had not set up a strong government structure? Write a brief essay presenting your point of view on this question. **HSS Analysis Skills CS 1, HI 1, HI 2, HI 3**

Interactive Reader and Study Guide

Section 5

MAIN IDEAS
1. Farming and manufacturing grew during the Han dynasty.
2. Trade routes linked China with the Middle East and Rome.
3. Buddhism came to China from India and gained many followers.

HSS 6.2
Students analyze the geographic, political, economic, religious, and social structures of the early civilizations of China.

Key Terms and People

silk a soft, light, highly valued fabric made from the cocoons of silkworms

Silk Road a network of routes between China and the Mediterranean Sea

diffusion the spread of ideas from one culture to another

Academic Vocabulary

procedure the way a task is accomplished

Section Summary

FARMING AND MANUFACTURING

During the Han dynasty, many farming advances led to bigger harvests. Manufacturing methods improved. Master ironworkers developed the iron plow and the wheelbarrow, two devices that made farming vastly more efficient.

The centuries-old process of producing **silk** increased. Weavers used foot-powered looms to weave silk threads into beautiful fabric. Garments made from silk were very expensive. The Chinese were determined to keep their **procedure** for making silk a secret. Revealing this secret was punishable by death.

TRADE ROUTES

When Han armies conquered lands deep in Central Asia, they learned that people even farther west

> Name two devices that made farming more efficient.
> _____
> _____
> _____

> Why do you think it was important to keep the silk production process a secret?
> _____
> _____
> _____

wanted silk. Han leaders saw that they could make
a profit by bringing silk to Central Asia and trading
the cloth for strong, sturdy Central Asian horses.
The Central Asian people would take the silk to the
west and trade it for products they wanted.

> **Aside from Rome, where did many of the items traded for silk come from?**
> _____
> _____

Traders used a series of overland routes known
as the **Silk Road** to take Chinese goods to distant
buyers. Although traveling the Silk Road was
difficult and risky, it was worth it. Silk was so
popular in Rome, for example, that China grew
wealthy just from trading with the Romans. Traders
returned to China with gold, silver, precious stones,
and horses.

BUDDHISM COMES TO CHINA

Over time, the Han government became less stable.
Life became violent and uncertain. In this climate,
Buddhist missionaries from India began to attract
attention.

> **What did Buddhism provide that other beliefs lacked?**
> _____
> _____

Buddhism seemed to provide more hope than
the traditional Chinese beliefs did. At first, Indian
Buddhists had trouble explaining their religion to
the Chinese. Then they used the ideas of Daoism
to help describe Buddhist beliefs. Before long,
Buddhism caught on in China with both the rich
and poor.

> **Underline the sentence that describes how the Indian Buddhists made their religion understandable to the Chinese.**

Buddhism's introduction to China is an example
of **diffusion**, the spread of ideas from one culture
to another. Chinese culture adopted Buddhism and
changed in response to the new faith.

CHALLENGE ACTIVITY

Critical Thinking: Drawing Inferences Do you think it was difficult to
keep the origin of silk and its production process a secret? Write a brief
story about a woman who wants to tell the secret and her fear of the
dire consequences. **HSS Analysis Skills HR 2, HI 4, HI 6**

The Hebrews and Judaism

HISTORY–SOCIAL SCIENCE STANDARDS
HSS 6.3 Students analyze the geographic, political, economic, religious, and social structures of the Ancient Hebrews.
HSS Analysis Skill HR 2 Distinguish fact from opinion in historical narratives and stories.

CHAPTER SUMMARY

1. God tells Abraham to leave Mesopotamia and move to Canaan (c. 2000 BC)	3. The Exodus—Moses leads the Jews out of slavery in Egypt (c. 1200 BC)	5. Jerusalem falls to the Chaldeans (c. 586 BC) Many Jews taken as slaves to Babylon	7. Jerusalem conquered by Rome (63 BC)	9. Second revolt fails, Rome forces all remaining Jews to leave Jerusalem (c. AD 130)
2. Jews move to Egypt due to famine in Canaan	4. King David conquers Canaan, establishes capital in Jerusalem (c. 1000 BC)	6. Persia conquers the Chaldeans (c. 530 BC) Some Jews spread throughout the Persian Empire, others return to Jerusalem and build the Second Temple	8. Jews revolt against Roman rule. Roman destroys the Second Temple (AD 70). Many Jews taken as slaves to Rome, others scattered to parts of the Roman Empire and Egypt	10. Jews migrate to the Mediterranean region and beyond. Jews who settle in Spain and Portugal become the Sephardim

COMPREHENSION AND CRITICAL THINKING

Use information from the graphic organizer to answer the following questions.

1. Explain Who was the first Jew in the Bible? What did God ask of him?

_____

_____

2. Identify Cause and Effect Why did so many Jews leave Jerusalem in the first century AD?

_____

_____

3. Evaluate How did the Diaspora affect Judaism?

_____

_____

4. Draw a Conclusion Which trip was the hardest one for Jews to make? Explain your answer.

_____

_____

The Hebrews and Judaism

MAIN IDEAS

1. Abraham and Moses led the Hebrews to Canaan and to a new religion.
2. Strong kings united the Israelites to fight off invaders.
3. Invaders conquered and ruled the Hebrews after their kingdom broke apart.
4. Some women in Hebrew society made great contributions to their history.

Key Terms and People

Abraham the biblical father of the Hebrew people

Moses Hebrew prophet who led the Jews from slavery in Egypt

Exodus the journey the Hebrews made from Egypt to Canaan, led by Moses

Ten Commandments moral code of laws that God handed down to Moses

David former outlaw who became king after the death of Saul, Israel's first king

Solomon David's son; became king of the Israelites

Diaspora the scattering of the Jews outside of Canaan

Section Summary

ABRAHAM AND MOSES LEAD THE HEBREWS

A people called the Hebrews (HEE-brooz) appeared in Southwest Asia sometime between 2000 and 1500 BC. Their writings describe the laws of their religion. The Hebrew Bible, or Torah, traces the Hebrews back to a man named **Abraham**. The Bible says that God told Abraham to leave his home. God promised to lead him to a new land and to make his children into a mighty nation. Abraham moved to Canaan (KAY-nuhn). The Hebrews lived there for many years.

> Circle the name of the people who appeared in Southwest Asia sometime between 2000 and 1500 BC.

> Underline the promise that God made to Abraham. Where did Abraham move?
>
> _____

Some Hebrews later moved to Egypt. In time Egypt's ruler, the pharaoh, made them slaves. In the 1200s BC, God then told a man named **Moses** to demand the Hebrews' freedom. The pharaoh agreed only after a series of plagues struck Egypt.

Moses led the Hebrews out of slavery in Egypt in a journey called the **Exodus**. The Hebrew Bible says that during this journey, God gave Moses two stone tablets with laws written on them, known as the **Ten Commandments**. The Hebrews were to worship only God and to value human life, self-control, and justice. The Hebrews reached Canaan after 40 years. They became the Israelites.

Why was Moses an important Hebrew leader?
_____
_____
_____
_____

KINGS UNITE THE ISRAELITES

A man named Saul fought the Philistines (FI-li-steenz) and became the first king of Israel. After Saul died, **David** became king. David was well-loved. He defeated the Philistines and made the city of Jerusalem Israel's capital. David's son **Solomon** (SAHL-uh-muhn) became king next around 965 BC. Solomon was a strong king. He built a great temple in Jerusalem.

What three basic values are emphasized in the Ten Commandments?
_____
_____
_____
_____

Circle the names of the first three kings of Israel. Which king built a temple to God?
_____
_____

INVADERS CONQUER AND RULE

Soon after Solomon's death in 930 BC, Israel split into two kingdoms, Israel and Judah (JOO-duh). The people of Judah were known as Jews. Over the centuries the Jewish people were often conquered and enslaved. The scattering of the Jews outside of Judah is known as the **Diaspora**. Jerusalem was conquered by the Greeks during the 330s BC. Judah regained independence for a time, but was conquered again in 63 BC, this time by the Romans.

WOMEN IN HEBREW SOCIETY

Men dominated Hebrew society, but some Hebrew women made great contributions to the culture.

CHALLENGE ACTIVITY

Critical Thinking: Drawing Inferences Write a set of ten commandments that reflects the responsibilities and rights of students and faculty for your school. **HSS Analysis Skills CR3, CR5, HI2, HI5**

The Hebrews and Judaism

Section 2

MAIN IDEAS

1. Beliefs in God, education, justice, and obedience anchor Jewish society.

2. Jewish beliefs are recorded in the Torah, the Hebrew Bible, and the Commentaries.

3. The Dead Sea Scrolls reveal many ancient Jewish beliefs.

4. The ideas of Judaism have helped shape later cultures.

 HSS 6.3
Students analyze the geographic, political, economic, religious, and social structures of the Ancient Hebrews

Key Terms and People

Judaism the religion of the Hebrews

monotheism belief in only one god

Torah the sacred text of Judaism

synagogue Jewish house of worship

prophets people said to receive messages from God to be taught to others

Talmud commentaries, stories, and folklore recorded to explain Jewish laws

Dead Sea Scrolls writings by Jews who lived about 2,000 years ago

Section Summary

JEWISH BELIEFS ANCHOR THEIR SOCIETY

Jewish society is founded upon their religion, **Judaism**. Judaism's main beliefs are beliefs in God, education, justice, and obedience.

Judaism is the oldest known religion to practice **monotheism**, the belief in only one God. The Jews believe that they are God's chosen people. The Jews say their history was guided through God's relationship with Abraham, Moses, and other leaders. Moral and religious laws, believed to be handed down from God, have guided Jewish society through their history and continue to do so today.

Besides the Ten Commandments, Jews believe that Moses recorded a whole set of laws governing Jewish behavior. These laws are called Mosaic law. These laws set down rules for everything including what to eat, when to work, and how to pray. Today

> Underline the four core values of Judaism.

> What is monotheism?
> _____
> _____
> _____

Interactive Reader and Study Guide

Section 2, *continued*

Orthodox Jews continue to follow all of the Mosaic laws. Reform Jews choose not to follow many of the ancient rules. Conservative Jews fall in between.

TEXTS LIST JEWISH BELIEFS

The laws and principles of Judaism are written down in sacred texts. The most important text is the **Torah**. The five books of the Torah record most of the laws and the history of Judaism until the death of Moses. Every **synagogue**, or place of Jewish worship, has at least one Torah.

> Circle the name of the most important sacred Jewish text.

The Torah is one of the three parts of the Hebrew Bible, or Tanakh (tah-NAKH). The second part contains messages from **prophets**, people who are said to receive messages directly from God. The third part is a collection of poems, songs, stories, lessons, and histories.

The **Talmud** is a collection of commentaries, folktales, and stories written by scholars. These are intended to help people understand and analyze the laws described in the Hebrew Bible.

> What is in the Talmud?
> _____
> _____
> _____
> _____

SCROLLS REVEAL PAST BELIEFS

Another set of ancient texts, the **Dead Sea Scrolls**, was discovered in 1947. These scrolls, written by Jewish scholars about 2,000 years ago, contain commentaries and stories, and offer more information about ancient Jewish life.

JUDAISM AND LATER CULTURES

Jewish ideas have helped shape two other major world religions, Christianity and Islam. The Ten Commandments are reflected in our laws and in modern society's rules of behavior.

CHALLENGE ACTIVITY

Critical Thinking: Drawing Inferences Pretend you are a writer contributing to a modern-day Talmud of American life. Write a short story illustrating how one of the Ten Commandments is still followed today. **HSS Analysis Skills CR1, CR2, CR3, CR5, HI2, HI3, HI5**

The Hebrews and Judaism

MAIN IDEAS

1. Revolt, defeat, and migration led to great changes in Jewish culture.

2. Because Jews settled in different parts of the world, two different cultural traditions formed.

3. Jewish traditions and holy days celebrate their traditions and religion.

 HSS 6.3
Students analyze the geographic, political, economic, religious, and social structures of the Ancient Hebrews.

Key Terms and People

Zealots Jews who rebelled against their Roman rulers

rabbis teachers who guide Jews in their religious lives

Passover a time for Jews to remember the Exodus

High Holy Days the two most sacred Jewish holidays, Rosh Hashanah and Yom Kippur

Section Summary

REVOLT, DEFEAT, AND MIGRATION

The teachings of Judaism helped unite the ancient Jews. But many Jews were unhappy with the Roman rule of Jerusalem. Tensions increased. Some Jews refused to obey Roman officials. In AD 66, a group called the **Zealots** (ze-LUHTS) led a rebellion against Rome. After four years of fierce fighting, the rebellion failed. The Jews' main temple was destroyed in AD 70. The Romans put down another Jewish rebellion 60 years later. After this uprising, Jews were banned from living in Jerusalem. So they migrated to other parts of the world.

> Underline when the Zealots revolted against Roman rule. Why did they revolt?
> _____
> _____
> _____
> _____

TWO CULTURAL TRADITIONS

Because Jews could not worship at a central temple anymore, their traditions changed. Everywhere Jews went, they built local temples. They also appointed **rabbis**, religious leaders responsible for teaching Judaism. Even with a similar culture and

> Underline the definition of a rabbi in your summary.

background, Jewish traditions grew differently depending on where they moved. Two major Jewish cultures developed that still exist today.

The Ashkenazim (ahsh-kuh-NAH-zuhm) are descended from Jews who moved to France, Germany, and Eastern Europe. These Jews maintained separate customs from the region's residents. They even developed their own language, called Yiddish.

The Sephardim (suh-FAHR-duhm) moved to Spain and Portugal. Unlike the Ashkenazim, these Jews mixed with their non-Jewish neighbors. This melding of language and culture produced a Jewish golden age in Spain and Portugal. Many Jews contributed to artistic achievement and scientific discovery.

> **What was the main difference between the Ashkenazim and the Sephardim?**
> _____
> _____
> _____
> _____
> _____

TRADITIONS AND HOLY DAYS

No matter where Jews live, common traditions and holy days help them maintain and celebrate their long history. Many of these holidays honor the Jews' freedom. **Passover**, for example, celebrates the Jews' flight from slavery in Egypt during the Exodus. Hanukkah commemorates the successful rededication of the Temple of Jerusalem during the successful revolt against the Greeks in 160 BC.

The most important holidays are the **High Holy Days**. These holy days are Rosh Hashanah (rahsh-uh-SHAH-nuh), which celebrates the Jewish New Year, and Yom Kippur (yohm-ki-POOHR), when Jews ask God to forgive their sins.

> **What is the proper name for the Jewish New Year?**
> _____
> _____

CHALLENGE ACTIVITY

Critical Thinking: Drawing Inferences Pretend that you are a Jew being forced to leave Jerusalem during Roman rule. Where would you go— Spain or Portugal, or Eastern Europe? Write a letter to your relatives explaining why you chose a particular place. Be sure to refer to the differences between the Ashkenazim and Sephardim. **HSS Analysis Skills HI2, CR1, CR5**

Ancient Greece

HISTORY–SOCIAL SCIENCE STANDARDS
HSS 6.4 Students analyze the geographic, political, economic, religious, and social structures of the early civilizations of ancient Greece.

CHAPTER SUMMARY

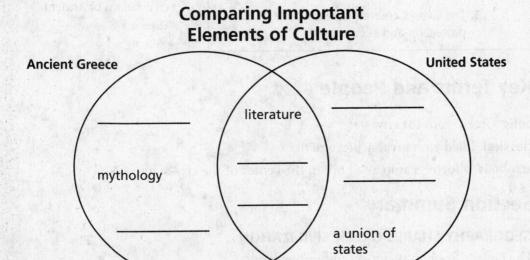

**Comparing Important
Elements of Culture**

Ancient Greece   United States

_____

literature

_____   _____

mythology

_____

_____   _____

_____   a union of
states

COMPREHENSION AND CRITICAL THINKING

Use the answers to the following questions to fill in the graphic
organizer above.

1. Explain How is U.S. culture similar to that of ancient Greece? How is it different?

_____

_____

2. Identify Cause and Effect When and why did the Greeks form city-states?

_____

_____

3. Evaluate How did democracy first develop in Athens?

_____

_____

4. Draw a Conclusion How did mythology influence the daily lives of Greeks?

_____

_____

Ancient Greece

MAIN IDEAS

1. Geography helped shape early Greek civilizations.
2. Trading cultures developed in the Minoan and Mycenaean civilizations.
3. The Greeks created city-states for protection and security.

 HSS 6.4

Students analyze the geographic, political, economic, religious, and social structures of the early civilizations of Ancient Greece.

Key Terms and People

polis Greek word for city-state

classical filled with great achievements

acropolis a fortress atop a tall hill in the center of the city-states

Section Summary

GEOGRAPHY SHAPES GREEK CIVILIZATION

The Greeks lived on rocky, mountainous lands, located on a peninsula surrounded by the Mediterranean, Ionian, and Aegean Seas. The peninsula has an irregular shape. Many islands float off the mainland. This area was the home of one of the world's greatest civilizations.

> Underline the names of the three seas that ringed the Greek peninsula.

The few small valleys and plains of Greece provided farmland and that is where people settled. These communities were separated by steep mountains, so there was little contact between groups. The villages created separate governments.

> Why did separate governments develop in ancient Greece?
>
> _____
> _____
> _____

Because they were surrounded by water the Greeks became skilled shipbuilders and sailors. The Greeks were exposed to other cultures when they sailed to other lands.

TRADING CULTURES DEVELOP

Of the many cultures that settled and grew in early Greece, the earliest and most influential were the Minoans and the Mycenaens. By 2000 BC these two cultures had built advanced societies on the

Interactive Reader and Study Guide

Section 1, *continued*

island of Crete. <u>The Minoans were known as the best shipbuilders of their time</u>. They used ships mainly for trading purposes. A volcano that erupted in the 1600s BC may have led to the end of the Minoan civilization.

> While the Minoans built _____,
>
> the Mycenaeans built _____.

The Mycenaeans spoke the language that became Greek. While the Minoans were sailing, the Mycenaeans were building fortresses on the Greek mainland. <u>The Mycenaeans eventually took over the trade routes once sailed by the Minoans</u>. The Mycenaeans set up a powerful trading network on the Mediterranean and Black seas. But Mycenaean culture also fell prey to earthquakes and invaders. Greece entered a dark period.

GREEKS CREATE CITY-STATES

After 300 years of war and disorder communities began to band together for stability and protection. They created the **polis**, or city-state. This marked the beginning of the Greek **classical** age, a time filled with great achievements.

> What features of the polis made it a safe, protected place to live and conduct business?
>
> _____
>
> _____
>
> _____

A city-state often was built around a fortress perched atop a high hill called an **acropolis**. Walls surrounded many of these cities. Much of daily life centered around the agora, or marketplace, where politics and shopping shared the stage. As stability returned some of the Greek city-states formed colonies in foreign lands. Early colonies included modern-day Istanbul in Turkey, Marseilles in France, and Naples in Italy. This created further independence for these city-states, and some city-states became great trading centers.

CHALLENGE ACTIVITY

Critical Thinking: Drawing Inferences You are a leader of an ancient Greek polis, or city-state, dealing with all the same problems and circumstances the real city-states of the time faced. Write your own set of laws that would improve both security and quality of life for the citizens who live there. **HSS Analysis Skills CS3, HI 1, HI 6**

Interactive Reader and Study Guide

Ancient Greece

MAIN IDEAS

1. Aristocrats and tyrants ruled early Athens.
2. Athens created the world's first democracy.
3. Ancient democracy was different than modern democracy.

 HSS 6.4
Students analyze the geographic, political, economic, religious, and social structures of the early civilizations of Ancient Greece.

Key Terms and People

democracy type of government in which people rule themselves

oligarchy government in which only a few people have power

aristocrats rich landowners

citizens people with the right to participate in government

tyrant leader who rules by the use of force

Pericles Athenian leader who ruled at the height of Athenian democracy

Section Summary

ARISTOCRATS AND TYRANTS RULE

Democracy was born in Ancient Greece in the city of Athens. Democracy is a form of a government in which people rule themselves. However, Athens was ruled first by kings, and then by an **oligarchy** of **aristocrats**, or rich landowners.

In the 600s BC a group of rebels tried to overthrow the aristocrats. The rebellion failed and Draco gained power in Athens. Draco was a strict leader and was very unpopular. His successor, Solon, ruled that all free men were **citizens** who had a right to participate in government. But it was too late; people were tired of the aristocracy.

Peisistratus overthrew the oligarchy and became a leader of Athens by force. Peisistratus was the first **tyrant**. Though that word has a negative meaning today, some Greek tyrants were good leaders. Peisistratus led well and Athens flourished under his care. But after he died rebellious aristocrats regained control of Athens.

> **Was democracy the only form of government in the ancient Greek city-states?**
> _____
> _____

> **Look up the word "draconian" in a dictionary. Write the definition here:**
> _____
> _____
> _____
> _____

ATHENS CREATES DEMOCRACY

A leader named Cleisthenes introduced democracy
to Athens in 500 BC. Though he was an aristocrat
himself, he did not support the aristocracy. He
overthrew the aristocratic leaders using popular
support. Under his rule all citizens had the right to
participate in the assembly that created laws. The
assemblies were held outdoors and anyone could
give a speech before votes were taken. This could be
messy. Either too many people would come to an
assembly or not enough. Eventually the Athenians
began to select city officials to make decisions.
Citizens were eventually allowed to decide court
cases by serving on juries.

> What do you think is the major disadvantage of allowing every citizen to participate in lawmaking?
> _____
> _____
> _____
> _____

Citizens gradually gained more power. Athenian
democracy reached its height with **Pericles**, who led
the government from 460 to 429 BC. Still, democracy
all but ended when Athens was conquered by
Macedonia in the 330s BC. The Macedonian king
did not like anyone other than himself making laws.
Though the city council kept operating in a limited
way, a new Greek king in 320 BC abolished even
that right.

ANCIENT DEMOCRACY DIFFERS FROM MODERN DEMOCRACY

Although citizenship was very limited, Athens had
a direct democracy, in which every citizen could
participate and the majority ruled.

The United States operates as a representative
government, in which citizens elect people to
represent them.

> Name an example of direct democracy practiced in the United States today.
> _____
> _____

CHALLENGE ACTIVITY

Critical Thinking: Drawing Inferences Have students in the class discuss
and vote on an issue—real or fictional—first as a direct democracy and
then as a representative democracy. Have them discuss the merits of
both democracies, or write a paper describing which system they prefer
and why. **HSS Analysis Skills HI 1, CR 5**

Interactive Reader and Study Guide

Ancient Greece

Section 3

<table>
<tr><td>

MAIN IDEAS

1. The Greeks created myths to explain the world.

2. Ancient Greek literature provides some of the world's greatest poems and stories.

3. Greek literature lives in and influences our world even today.

</td></tr>
</table>

 HSS 6.4

Students analyze the geographic, political, economic, religious, and social structures of the early civilizations of Ancient Greece.

Key Terms and People

mythology body of stories about gods or heroes that tries to explain how the world works

Homer author of two great epic poems, the *Iliad* and the *Odyssey*

Sappho most famous lyrical poet of ancient Greece

Aesop author of the world's most famous set of fables

fables short stories that offer lessons on living

Section Summary

MYTHS EXPLAIN THE WORLD

Instead of science the ancient Greeks used **mythology**—stories about gods or heroes—to try to explain how the world works. The Greeks believed that the gods caused natural events, from the rising of the moon to thunderstorms. Everything was attributed to the gods, from disasters to daily events.

The Greeks believed that Demeter, the goddess of agriculture, caused the seasons. Hades, the god of the underworld, kidnapped Demeter's daughter. Demeter struck a bargain to get her daughter back for half of the year, during the spring and summer. In the winter, she missed her daughter, and because of her grief the plants did not grow.

Some myths told not of gods, but of heroes. Each city had its own hero, real or fictional, who would slay terrible monsters. The most famous Greek hero was Hercules. The Greeks loved to tell these stories.

> We often use the word "myth" as a synonym for "lie" or "untruth." Do you believe this is correct? Explain your answer.
>
> _____
> _____
> _____
> _____

> Is the story of Demeter worthless because it conflicts with the scientific explanation of seasonal change? Why or why not?
>
> _____
> _____
> _____

Interactive Reader and Study Guide

ANCIENT GREEK LITERATURE

Because of their love of stories, Greek writers produced great works of literature and some of the world's most famous stories. Among the earliest and most influential are the epic poems the *Iliad* and the *Odyssey*, by the poet **Homer**. It is thought that Homer lived some time during the 800s–700s BC. Scholars are not sure if Homer actually existed, but the poems were central to Greek lore and education. The *Iliad* told the story of the Myceaneans' war with the Trojans. The *Odyssey* told of the Greek hero Odysseus' long journey home after the war.

> What form of literature are the *Iliad* and the *Odyssey*?
> _____
> _____

Other forms of literature were also popular. Lyric poetry, recited by the poet while playing the lyre, was especially prized. The most famous lyric poet was a woman, **Sappho**. Fables, or short stories that offer the readers lessons on life, were also popular. The most famous fable writer was **Aesop**, who was said to live sometime before 400 BC. Aesop's fables are still commonly told today.

> Who was Sappho?
> _____
> _____

GREEK LITERATURE LIVES

Greek literature, language, and art have had a great influence on modern culture. The English language is peppered with Greek expressions: a long journey, for example, is called an "odyssey" after Odysseus. Many places are named after Greek gods. Greek myths and stories have inspired painters, writers, and filmmakers for centuries.

> The Greek word for people is "demos." What political system is known in English by a word derived from "demos"?
> _____
> _____

CHALLENGE ACTIVITY

Critical Thinking: Drawing Inferences The later Greeks believed that their greatest literary works from earlier times were written by individual authors. Historical evidence suggests that these early works actually represented stories that evolved and changed with successive generations of poets. Write a paragraph describing why scholars might doubt the existence of writers like Homer and Aesop. **HSS Analysis Skills CR 1, CR 2, CR 3, CR 4**

Name _____ Class _____ Date _____

The Greek World

HISTORY-SOCIAL SCIENCE STANDARDS
HSS 6.4 Students analyze the geographic, political, economic, religious, and social structures of the early civilization of Ancient Greece.
HSS Analysis Skill HI 1 Explain central issues and problems from the past.
HSS Analysis Skill HI 2 Understand and distinguish sequence.

CHAPTER SUMMARY

> Persia invades Greece

> Athens-Sparta alliance victorious

> Peloponnesian War between Athens and Sparta

> Athenian culture flourishes

> Alexander the Great captures Athens

> Alexander's empire grows

> Hellenistic culture flourishes

> Rome engulfs Greece, Syria, and Egypt

COMPREHENSION AND CRITICAL THINKING

Use information from the graphic organizer to answer the following questions.

1. Recall Which ruler can be regarded as the founder of Hellenistic culture?

_____

2. Draw Inferences Why did the very different cultures of Athens and Sparta form an alliance?

_____

3. Evaluate Why do you think Athens surrendered so quickly to Alexander?

_____

4. Identify Which new major power put an end to Hellenistic culture?

_____

Section 1

MAIN IDEAS

1. Persia became an empire under Cyrus the Great.
2. The Persian Empire grew stronger under Darius I.
3. The Persians fought Greece twice in the Persian Wars.

 HSS 6.4
Students analyze the geographic, political, economic, religious, and social structures of the early civilization of Ancient Greece.

Key Terms and People

cavalry a unit of soldiers mounted on horses

Cyrus the Great founder of the Persian Empire

Darius I Persian emperor who organized and expanded the empire

Persian Wars a series of wars between Persia and Greece beginning in 490 BC

Xerxes I Persian emperor who led the second invasion of Greece in 480 BC

Section Summary

PERSIA BECOMES AN EMPIRE

Early in their history, the Persians often fought other peoples of Southwest Asia. In 550 BC the Persian king Cyrus II won independence from a group called the Medes. He went on to conquer almost all of Southwest Asia. His well-organized army included many war chariots and a powerful **cavalry**. Cyrus let the people he conquered keep their own customs. As a result, few people rebelled and the empire remained strong. By the time he died around 529 BC, Cyrus ruled the largest empire the world had ever seen. He became known in history as **Cyrus the Great**.

> Why did few people rebel against Cyrus's rule?
> _____
> _____

> Why do you think king Cyrus became known as "the Great"?
> _____
> _____
> _____
> _____

THE PERSIAN EMPIRE GROWS STRONGER

Darius I seized power when the death of Cyrus's son left Persia without a clear leader. Darius organized the empire by dividing it into 20 provinces. Then he chose governors called satraps (SAY-traps) to rule the provinces for him.

Darius expanded the Persian Empire eastward to the Indus Valley and westward into Southeastern Europe. He called himself king of kings to remind other rulers of his power.

Darius's many improvements to Persian society included roads. Messengers used these roads to travel quickly throughout Persia. Darius also built a new capital called Persepolis.

During his reign a popular new religion called Zoroastrianism (zawr-uh-WAS-tree-uh-nih-zuhm) arose in Persia. This religion taught that the forces of good and evil were fighting for control of the universe.

> Do you think the Zoroastrian teaching is still relevant today? Why or why not?
> _____
> _____
> _____
> _____
> _____

THE PERSIANS FIGHT GREECE

In 499 BC several Greek cities in what is now Turkey rebelled against Persian rule. They were joined by a few city-states from mainland Greece. The Persians put down the revolt, but nine years later Darius invaded Greece and began the **Persian Wars**. The Greeks won the first battle, at Marathon, because they had better weapons and armor.

> Circle the sentence that explains why the Greeks defeated the Persians at the Battle of Marathon.

Ten years later, Persian Emperor **Xerxes I** (ZUHRK-seez) sent another army into Greece. The city-states of Athens and Sparta joined forces to defend Greece. Despite a brave stand by the Spartans at Thermopylae (thuhr-MAH-puh-lee), the Persians succeeded in attacking and burning Athens. However in the subsequent battles of Salamis (SAH-luh-muhs) and Plataea (pluh-TEE-uh), the Greeks prevailed and brought an end to the wars. They had defeated a powerful foe and defended their homeland.

> Who won the Persian Wars?

CHALLENGE ACTIVITY

Critical Thinking: Drawing Inferences Draw a simple map of a location where three armed soldiers could prevent an entire army of foot-soldiers from moving forward. **HSS Analysis Skills HI 2, HI 4**

The Greek World

Section 2

MAIN IDEAS

1. The Spartans built a military society to provide security and protection.

2. The Athenians admired the mind and the arts in addition to physical abilities.

3. Sparta and Athens fought over who should have power and influence in Greece.

 HSS 6.4
Students analyze the geographic, political, economic, religious, and social structures of the early civilization of Ancient Greece.

Key Terms and People

alliance an agreement to work together

Peloponnesian War a war between the two great Greek city-states of Athens and Sparta in the 400s BC

Section Summary

SPARTA BUILDS A MILITARY SOCIETY

Spartan life was dominated by the army. Courage and strength were the highest values. Unhealthy babies were taken outside the city and left to die. Boys who survived were trained from an early age to be soldiers. Boys ran, jumped, swam, and threw javelins to increase their strength. Men between the ages of 20 and 30 lived in army barracks and only occasionally visited their families. Spartan men stayed in the army until they turned 60.

Because Spartan men were often away at war, Spartan women had more rights than other Greek women. Women owned much of the land in Sparta and ran their households. Women also learned how to run, jump, wrestle, and throw javelins, and even competed with men in sporting events.

Slaves grew the city's crops and did many other jobs. Although slaves outnumbered Spartan citizens, fear of the army kept them from rebelling.

Sparta was officially ruled by two kings who jointly led the army. But elected officials ran

> Look up the word *Spartan* in a dictionary. Does it mean more than simply "having to do with Sparta"? Write that meaning here.
>
> _____
> _____
> _____
> _____
> _____

> How was women's treatment in Sparta different from their treatment in the rest of Greece?
>
> _____
> _____
> _____
> _____

Sparta's day-to-day activities and handled dealings between Sparta and other city-states.

ATHENIANS ADMIRE THE MIND

Sparta's main rival in Greece was Athens. Although Athens had a powerful military and valued physical training, the Athenians also prized education, clear thinking, and the arts. They believed that studying the arts made people better citizens.

> Underline the sentence that explains why the Athenians valued the arts.

In addition to physical training, many Athenian students learned to read, write, and count as well as sing and play musical instruments. Boys from rich families often had private tutors who taught them philosophy, geometry, astronomy, and other subjects, as well as public speaking. Boys from poor families, however, did not receive much education and girls got almost none. Despite Athens' reputation for freedom and democracy, Athenian women had almost no rights at all.

> Why do you think public speaking was considered an important part of the education of rich boys?
> _____
> _____
> _____

SPARTA AND ATHENS FIGHT

After the Persian Wars, many Greek city-states joined an **alliance** to help defend each other and protect trade. With its navy protecting the islands, Athens was the most powerful member of the league. Soon Athenians began to treat other city-states as their subjects. In 431 BC Sparta and other cities formed a league of their own and declared war on Athens. In the long **Peloponnesian War** that followed the Athenians won at first, but were forced to surrender in 404 BC. For about 30 years after this the Spartans controlled nearly all of Greece, but resentment from other city-states led to a long period of war that weakened all of Greece and left it open to attack from outside.

> Circle the noun that describes the popular feeling that undermined the power of Sparta.

CHALLENGE ACTIVITY

Critical Thinking: Drawing Inferences Write a poem or a song expressing how it feels when someone you love goes to fight in a war.
HSS Analysis Skills HR 5, HI 1

The Greek World

MAIN IDEAS

1. Macedonia conquered Greece in the 300s BC.

2. Alexander the Great built an empire that united much of Europe, Asia, and Egypt.

3. The Hellenistic kingdoms formed from Alexander's empire blended Greek and other cultures.

 HSS 6.4
Students analyze the geographic, political, economic, religious, and social structures of the early civilization of Ancient Greece.

Key Terms and People

Philip II powerful king of Macedonia

phalanx a group of warriors who stood close together in a square

Alexander the Great king of Macedonia who built the largest empire the world had ever seen

Hellenistic name for the blended culture that developed in Alexander's empire

Section Summary

MACEDONIA CONQUERS GREECE

About 360 BC **Philip II** of Macedonia invaded Athens and won easily. The rest of Greece surrendered. Philip's victory resulted from his military strategy and weaponry. For instance, he extended the Greek idea of the **phalanx** by giving each soldier a spear 16 feet long. Philip planned to conquer Persia, but he was murdered in 336 BC and his throne passed to his 20-year-old son Alexander.

> Why do you think Philip's improvement on the phalanx gave his armies an advantage in battle?
>
> _____
> _____
> _____
> _____

ALEXANDER BUILDS AN EMPIRE

When Philip died, the people in the Greek city of Thebes rebelled. Alexander attacked Thebes and enslaved the Theban people. He used Thebes as an example of what would happen if any other Greek cities rebelled against him. Alexander went on to defeat the Persians time after time and to conquer Egypt. He became ruler of what had been the

> About what age was Alexander when his army attacked Thebes and enslaved the Thebans?

Interactive Reader and Study Guide

Persian empire. Before his death at 33 years of age, **Alexander the Great** (as he came to be called) had built an empire stretching from the Adriatic Sea west to India and to the Upper Nile in the south.

Alexander admired Greek culture and worked to spread Greek influence by founding cities in the lands he conquered. He encouraged Greek settlers to move to these new cities and as a result, Greek became a common language throughout Alexander's empire. Even as he supported the spread of Greek culture, however, Alexander encouraged common people to keep their own customs and traditions. The new, blended culture that developed is called **Hellenistic**. It was not purely Greek, but it was heavily influenced by Greek ideas.

> Underline the sentence that explains why Greek became a common language throughout Alexander's empire.

> Why is Hellenistic culture called a "blended" culture?
> _____
> _____
> _____
> _____

HELLENISTIC KINGDOMS

Alexander died unexpectedly without an obvious heir. With no clear direction, his generals fought for power. Eventually, three distinct Hellenistic kingdoms emerged: Macedonia (which included Greece), Syria, and Egypt. Although Hellenistic culture flourished in all three kingdoms—in particular, Alexandria in Egypt became a great center of culture and learning—all three kingdoms fell to the growing power of Rome between 60 and 30 BC.

> What new empire was growing in power during the 100s BC?
> _____
> _____

CHALLENGE ACTIVITY

Critical Thinking: Drawing Inferences Write a short essay that characterizes the United States as having a blended culture. **HSS Analysis Skills HI 1, HI2, HI 3**

Name _____ Class _____ Date _____

The Greek World

Section 4

MAIN IDEAS

1. The Greeks made great contributions to the arts.
2. The teachings of Socrates, Plato, and Aristotle are the basis of modern philosophy.
3. In science, the Greeks made key discoveries in math, medicine, and engineering.

 HSS 6.4
Students analyze the geographic, political, economic, religious, and social structures of the early civilization of Ancient Greece.

Key Terms and People

Socrates the first of the great Greek thinkers and teachers

Plato teacher and thinker, student of Socrates, and founder of the Academy

Aristotle philosopher who taught that people should live lives of moderation based on reason

reason clear and ordered thinking

Euclid great and influential mathematician

Hippocrates great Greek doctor who taught how to treat disease by understanding what caused illness

Section Summary

THE ARTS

The ancient Greeks were master artists. Their paintings and statues have been admired for hundreds of years. Greek sculptors studied the human body, especially how it looks when it is moving. They used what they learned when they made their statues. Greek artists painted detailed scenes on vases, pots, and other vessels. The remains of Greek architecture show how much care the Greeks took in designing their buildings so they would reflect the beauty of their cities.

Greek writers created new literary forms, including drama and history. Dramatists wrote tragedies, which described hardships faced by Greek heroes, and comedies, which made fun of people and ideas.

> **Which three art forms are mentioned in this paragraph?**
> _____
> _____
> _____
> _____

Interactive Reader and Study Guide

Historians were interested in the lessons that history could teach. They tried to figure out what caused wars so the Greeks could learn from their mistakes and avoid similar wars in the future.

PHILOSOPHY

The ancient Greeks worshipped gods and goddesses whose actions explained many of the mysteries of the world. But around 500 BC a few people began to think about other explanations. We call these people philosophers. Philosophers believe in the power of the human mind to think, explain, and understand life.

> Look in a dictionary for the etymology (word origin) of the word "philosophy."

Socrates (SAHK-ruh-teez) believed that people must never stop looking for knowledge. He taught by asking questions. When people answered, he challenged their answers with more questions. His student **Plato** (PLAYT-oh) created a school called the Academy to which students, philosophers, and scientists could come to discuss ideas. Plato's student **Aristotle** (ar-uh-STAH-tuhl) taught that people should live lives of moderation, or balance. He believed that moderation was based on **reason**. Aristotle also made great advances in the field of logic, the process of making inferences.

> Would Socrates say that we stop learning when we leave school? What would he say?
> _____
> _____
> _____
> _____

SCIENCE

Many of the rules we still use today to measure and calculate were first developed by Greek mathematicians like **Euclid** (YOO-kluhd). Greek doctors like **Hippocrates** (hip-AHK-ruh-teez) wanted to cure diseases and keep people healthy. Greek inventors also made many discoveries that are still in use, from practical devices like water screws (which bring water up from a lower level to a higher one) to playful mechanical toys.

> Do you think doctors today have the same fundamental beliefs about medicine as Hippocrates did? Why or why not?
> _____
> _____
> _____
> _____

CHALLENGE ACTIVITY

Critical Thinking: Drawing Inferences Write a story, poem, or play that makes fun of some well-known figure. **HSS Analysis Skills HR 2, HR 3, HR 5**

The Roman Republic

HISTORY–SOCIAL SCIENCE STANDARDS
HSS 6.7 Students analyze the geographic, political, economic, religious, and social structures during the development of Rome.
HSS Analysis Skill CS 1 Understand how events are related in time.
HSS Analysis Skill CS 2 Construct time lines.

CHAPTER SUMMARY

Patrician	Plebeian	The poor	Slave
wealthy	gained some political power	could not join the army	had no legal rights
original Roman Senate member	could eventually serve in a political position	could not vote	considered property of the wealthy
had most of the political power	could serve in the army	had very few rights	
could serve in any political position	could not marry a patrician		
could vote	later got the vote		

COMPREHENSION AND CRITICAL THINKING

Use information from the graphic organizer to answer the following questions.

1. Explain What class of people originally held all of the political power in Rome?

_____

2. Identify Cause and Effect Why did the patricians change the government and allow plebeians to run for political office?

_____

_____

3. Evaluate Who did not have the right to vote or participate in politics? Why?

_____

_____

4. Draw a Conclusion Was Rome a fair place for most people who lived there, or were other ancient civilizations better? Why or why not?

_____

_____

The Roman Republic

Section 1

MAIN IDEAS

1. The geography of Italy made land travel difficult but helped the Romans prosper.
2. Ancient historians were very interested in Rome's legendary history.
3. Once a monarchy, the Romans created a republic.

 HSS 6.7
Students analyze the geographic, political, economic, religious, and social structures during the development of Rome.

Key Terms and People

Aeneas mythical hero who fled the fallen city of Troy for Italy in a journey chronicled in Virgil's *Aeneid*

Romulus and Remus mythical twin brothers who are said to have founded Rome

republic government led by rulers elected by the citizens

dictator ruler with almost absolute power, elected during time of war

Cincinnatus famous dictator who chose not to retain his power

plebeians Rome's common people, including artisans, craftsmen, and traders

patricians wealthy, noble people of Rome

Section Summary

THE GEOGRAPHY OF ITALY

Rome grew from a small town on the Tiber River to become a great power. Rome conquered Greece, Mesopotamia, Egypt, and Persia. Rome's central location and good climate were factors in its success. Because most of Italy is surrounded by water, Romans could easily travel by sea. The mountains in the north made it difficult to travel over land. The warm dry weather resulted in high crop yields, so the Romans had plenty of food.

> Why did Italy's geography help the rise of Rome?
> _____
> _____
> _____

ROME'S LEGENDARY ORIGINS

Rome's beginnings are a mystery. A few ancient ruins show that people lived there as early as 800 BC. Later, the Romans wanted a glorious past, so they created stories or legends about their history.

> Why did the Romans make up stories and legends about their history?
> _____
> _____
> _____

The early Romans believed their history began with the mythical hero **Aeneas** (i-NEE-uhs). Aeneas fled Troy when the Greeks destroyed the city during the Trojan War. He formed an alliance with a group called the Latins and traveled to Italy. This story is told in the *Aeneid* (i-NEE-id), an epic poem written by a poet named Virgil (VUHR-juhl) around 20 BC.

According to legend, Rome was built by twin brothers **Romulus** (RAHM-yuh-luhs) and **Remus** (REE-muhs). Romulus killed Remus and became the first king of Rome. Scholars believe Rome started sometime between 800 and 700 BC. Early Rome was ruled by kings until the Romans created a **republic** in 509 BC.

> **Why is Aeneas sometimes referred to as "the Father of Rome?"**
> _____
> _____
> _____

> **Which of the two brothers named the city of Rome after himself?**
> _____
> _____

THE EARLY REPUBLIC

In the republic the Romans created, citizens elected leaders to govern them. They voted once a year to prevent any one person from gaining too much power. But early Rome had its troubles. For one thing, Rome was usually at war with nearby countries.

To lead the country during war, the Romans elected **dictators**, rulers with almost absolute power. A dictator's power could not last more than six months. The most famous dictator was **Cincinnatus** (sin-suh-NAT-uhs), a farmer elected to defeat a major enemy. He resigned as dictator right after the war and went back to his farm.

Within Rome the **plebeians**, or common people, worked for change. Only the city's **patricians**, the wealthy citizens, could be elected to rule Rome. When the plebeians elected a council, the patricians changed the government.

> **Why do you think Rome's patricians were so concerned when the plebeians elected their own council?**
> _____
> _____
> _____
> _____

CHALLENGE ACTIVITY

Critical Thinking: Drawing Inferences You are a Roman plebeian. Write a campaign speech saying why people should elect you to office—even though your position has no official power. Create a historically accurate persona. **HSS Analysis Skills CR 5, HI 1**

MAIN IDEAS

1. Roman government was made up of three parts that worked together to run the city.
2. Written laws helped keep order in Rome.
3. The Roman Forum was the heart of Roman society.

 HSS 6.7
Students analyze the geographic, political, economic, religious, and social structures during the development of Rome.

Key Terms and People

magistrates officials elected to fulfill specific duties for the city
consuls most powerful elected officials in the Roman Republic
Roman Senate a powerful group of wealthy citizens who advised elected officials
veto to prohibit an official action
Latin language spoken by the ancient Romans
checks and balances methods of balancing power
forum Rome's public meeting place

Section Summary

ROMAN GOVERNMENT

During the 400s BC, the plebeians were unhappy that they did not have any say with the government. The city's leaders knew that they had to compromise or the plebeians might rise up and overthrow the government. So the patricians created positions in the government for the plebeians. A tripartite (try-PAHR-tyt) government, a government with three parts, was established to keep any one group from getting too much power.

The first part of the government was made up elected officials called **magistrates** (MA-juh-strayts). The most powerful magistrates were called **consuls** (KAHN-suhlz). Two consuls were elected each year to run the city and lead the army. The consuls got advice from the **Roman Senate**. The Senate was a council of wealthy, powerful citizens who held seats for life. Magistrates who finished their one-year terms

Why do you think it is important to keep too much power from concentrating among one group of people?

_____
_____
_____

What is the difference between a consul and a magistrate?

_____
_____
_____

Interactive Reader and Study Guide

earned a seat on the Senate, so the Senate gained more power as time passed.

The third branch of government had two parts. The first branch was made up of assemblies. The assemblies elected the magistrates who ran the city of Rome. The second branch was a group of officials called tribunes. The tribunes had the power to **veto** (VEE-toh), or prohibit, actions by the government. Veto means "to forbid" in **Latin**, the ancient Roman language.

> Underline the definition of the Latin word "veto."

Checks and balances existed to even out power. Some officials had the power to block actions by other officials. Action could be stalled if people could not work together. But when an agreement was reached, Rome worked strongly and efficiently.

WRITTEN LAWS KEEP ORDER

At first Rome's laws were not written down. People thought that it was not fair to be charged by laws they did not know existed. In 450 BC Rome's first legal code was written on twelve bronze tablets and displayed in the **forum**, Rome's public meeting place. Although the Romans continued to make laws, the Law of the Twelve Tables remained as the basis of Roman law.

> What was the official name of Rome's first set of written laws?
>
> _____
> _____
> _____

THE ROMAN FORUM

The forum was the heart of Rome. All the important government buildings and religious temples were there. It was also the main meeting place for Roman citizens. It was used for public speeches, and for shopping and entertainment.

> Do you think our modern idea of "downtown" is related to the idea of the Roman Forum? Why or why not?
>
> _____
> _____
> _____
> _____

CHALLENGE ACTIVITY

Critical Thinking: Drawing Inferences Do some research and locate the text of the Roman law code of 450 BC. Which laws do you think were fair and which laws do you think were unfair? Remove and change any unfair laws, explaining how and why you made the changes. Discuss whether those laws, including the amended ones, should or should not apply to the modern world. **HSS Analysis Skills CS 3, HI 3**

The Roman Republic

MAIN IDEAS

1. The late republic period saw the growth of territory and trade.
2. Through wars, Rome grew beyond Italy.
3. Several crises struck the republic in its later years.

 HSS 6.7

Students analyze the geographic, political, economic, religious, and social structures during the development of Rome.

Key Terms and People

legions groups of up to 6,000 soldiers

Punic Wars a series of wars between Rome and Carthage

Hannibal brilliant Carthaginian general who attacked the city of Rome

Gaius Marius general who tried to solve unemployment by inviting poor people to join the army, creating a force more loyal to him than to Rome

Lucius Cornelius Sulla rival of Marius who raised his own army to defeat Marius and take control of Rome

Spartacus slave and former gladiator who led an uprising of slaves

Section Summary

GROWTH OF TERRITORY AND TRADE

Rome expanded due to threats from other cities. When the Gauls took over Rome in 410 BC, Roman officials paid them to leave. Because of this Rome was constantly fighting off invaders. Rome's army was very organized, so defense of the city was usually successful. Soldiers were divided into **legions**, or groups of up to 6,000 men. Each legion was divided into centuries, or groups of 100 soldiers. The army had the flexibility to fight together, or break up into smaller groups.

What is the military advantage of an army with both small units and large units?

_____

_____

_____

_____

Most Romans were originally farmers. Many of them moved to the city and ran their farms from afar with help from slaves. As the population of the city grew, so did the need for more food. An extensive trading network was established. Rome coined copper and silver money, which was used widely in the region.

What necessity led to the expansion of trade in ancient Rome?

_____

_____

ROME GROWS BEYOND ITALY

Rome's growth made both allies and enemies in the Mediterranean. The Roman army fought many wars, including the **Punic** (PYOO-nik) **Wars** with Carthage. Carthage was the capital of a Phoenician civilization that flourished in North Africa between 264 and 156 BC. Although an attack on Rome led by the brilliant general **Hannibal** nearly succeeded, Rome eventually conquered Carthage. The Romans then took over Gaul, Greece, and parts of Asia. The Romans were deeply influenced by the Greeks and adopted much of the Greek culture.

> **What body of water lay between Rome and Carthage?**
> _____
> _____

CRISES STRIKE THE REPUBLIC

As Rome's territory grew, so did its problems. Tensions between the rich and poor grew. Some leaders tried to keep the poor citizens happy, but their plans were not popular with the wealthy. Politicians who tried to make a change and went against Rome's powerful leaders were killed.

Army general **Gaius Marius** (GY-uhs MER-ee-uhs) encouraged the poor and the unemployed to join the army. Before, only people who owned property had been allowed in the army. As a result, the army became more loyal to Marius than to the Roman government.

> **Why do you think the poor and unemployed respected Gaius Marius?**
> _____
> _____
> _____

Another man, **Lucius Cornelius Sulla** (LOO-shuhs kawr-NEEL-yuhs SUHL-uh), raised his own army. He fought and killed Marius and became dictator. Soon afterward, **Spartacus** (SPAHR-tuh-kuhs), a slave and former gladiator, led an uprising of thousands of slaves against the republic. Spartacus was eventually defeated and killed, but these conflicts had weakened Rome.

> **Why do you think Spartacus attracted such a large following?**
> _____
> _____
> _____

CHALLENGE ACTIVITY

Critical Thinking: Drawing Inferences Spartacus was eventually caught and killed, yet his rebellion had an impact on Roman history. Write an essay evaluating how one person can affect the course of history, using Spartacus as an example. **HSS Analysis Skills HI 1, CS 1**

The Roman Empire

HISTORY–SOCIAL SCIENCE STANDARDS
HSS 6.7 Students analyze the geographic, political, economic, religious, and social structures during the development of Rome.
HSS Analysis Skill CS 3 Students use a variety of maps and documents to identify physical and cultural features of neighborhoods, cities, states, and countries, and to explain the historical migration of people, expansion and disintegration of empires, and the growth of economic systems.

CHAPTER SUMMARY

Science and engineering	led to	vault
Architecture	led to	
Art	led to	
Literature	led to	
Language	led to	Romance languages

COMPREHENSION AND CRITICAL THINKING

Use the answers to the following questions to fill in the graphic organizer above.

1. Describe Give one example of Roman architecture, one example of Roman art, and one example of Roman literature.

_____

_____

2. Draw a Conclusion How did the invention of the vault help the Romans create the Colosseum?

_____

_____

3. Evaluate In which field did the Romans differ most from the Greeks? Explain.

_____

_____

The Roman Empire

MAIN IDEAS

1. Romans called for change in their government.

2. Julius Caesar rose to power and became the sole ruler of Rome.

3. Augustus became Rome's first emperor after defeating Caesar's killers and his own former allies.

 HSS 6.7

Students analyze the geographic, political, economic, religious, and social structures during the development of Rome.

Key Terms and People

Cicero gifted speaker who called for improvements in the Roman government

orator public speaker

Julius Caesar the greatest general in Roman history

Pompey powerful Roman who was first a friend and then an enemy of Caesar

Marc Antony one of two leaders who took control of Rome after Caesar's death

Augustus Caesar's adopted son, who defeated Antony and Cleopatra and became Rome's sole ruler

Section Summary

THE CALL FOR CHANGE

Cicero, a famous **orator**, asked Romans to work together to limit the power of the generals and return all power to the Senate. Cicero wanted to bring order back to Rome. The republic was in chaos, but many Romans disagreed with Cicero. Rome's government stayed the same.

> **What actions did Cicero ask Romans to take?**
>
> _____
>
> _____

CAESAR'S RISE TO POWER

Julius Caesar was admired by Romans for his battle skills and courage. His soldiers respected him because he treated them well. Between 58 and 50 BC Caesar conquered nearly all of Gaul, consisting of much of modern France, Germany, northern Italy, and part of Britain. He made an alliance with the powerful **Pompey**. After Caesar had conquered Gaul, Pompey's allies told Caesar to give up his

> **What three things helped Caesar conquer Gaul?**
>
> _____
>
> _____

armies and come back to Rome. Instead, Caesar entered Rome with his army. Pompey and his allies fled. Pompey and his forces were driven into Egypt, where he was killed.

In Egypt Caesar became an ally of Queen Cleopatra. Caesar then returned to Rome and was named dictator for life. Many Senators turned against Caesar. On March 15, 44 BC, a group of Senators, including Caesar's friend Brutus, stabbed Caesar to death in the Senate house.

> **Why might many Senators have turned against Caesar?**
> _____
> _____

AUGUSTUS THE EMPEROR

Caesar's assassination shocked Romans. Many had loved him. **Marc Antony** and Octavian, later renamed **Augustus**, took charge of Roman politics. They led an army that defeated Brutus and their other opponents, who killed themselves after the final battle. Then Octavian returned to Italy while Antony headed east to fight Rome's enemies.

> **Why might Brutus have killed himself after the final battle?**
> _____
> _____

In Egypt Antony met Cleopatra and they fell in love. Cleopatra declared Antony king of Egypt and her co-ruler. Antony divorced his wife, who was Octavian's sister. Octavian viewed the divorce as an insult to his sister and to him. In 31 BC Octavian sent a fleet to attack Antony. In the Battle of Actium, Antony's fleet was beaten. Antony escaped to Egypt and was reunited with Cleopatra. They killed themselves to avoid capture by Octavian.

> **Circle the two sentences that best explain why Octavian sent a fleet to attack Antony.**

After Antony died Octavian became the sole ruler of Rome. He said he was working to bring back the republic, but he gained almost total power. He assumed the title *princeps*, which means first citizen. In 27 BC Octavian claimed that he was giving up all his power to the Senate. However, he took the name of Augustus and became the Roman emperor.

> **Why might Octavian have first assumed the title of *princeps*?**
> _____
> _____

CHALLENGE ACTIVITY

Critical Thinking: Summarizing Summarize the events leading from Caesar's conquest of Gaul to Octavian's becoming Roman emperor. **HSS Analysis Skills HI 2**

Interactive Reader and Study Guide

The Roman Empire

Section 2

MAIN IDEAS

1. The Roman Empire expanded to control the entire Mediterranean world.
2. Trade increased in Rome, both within the empire and with other people.
3. The Pax Romana was a period of peace and prosperity in the cities and the country.

HSS 6.7

Students analyze the geographic, political, economic, religious, and social structures during the development of Rome.

Key Terms and People

Hadrian the emperor under whom the Romans conquered most of the island of Britain

provinces the areas outside of Italy that the Romans controlled

currency money

Pax Romana the Roman Peace, a peaceful period in Rome's history

villas country homes belonging to rich Romans

Section Summary

THE EMPIRE EXPANDS

Rome ruled most of the Mediterranean world when it became an empire. Within 150 years the Roman Empire controlled large areas of Europe, Africa, and Asia. It was one of the largest empires in history. The Romans conquered some territories because they threatened to attack Rome. They overcame others to gain their gold, good farmlands, or other resources.

> Why did the Romans conquer so many territories?
> _____
> _____

The Romans ruled Gaul and much of central Europe by the 100s. **Hadrian** encountered a tough fight from the Celts, the people of Britain, but the Roman army drove them north. The Romans had also taken over Asia Minor, the eastern coast of the Mediterranean, and all of the northern African coast. Romans called the Mediterranean Mare Nostrum, meaning "Our Sea."

> Why did Romans call the Mediterranean *Mare Nostrum*?
> _____
> _____

The Romans met many new people as their empire expanded. Traders found that foreign goods

Interactive Reader and Study Guide

appealed to the Romans. They traveled to the
provinces to bring back metals, cloth, and food. In
return the Romans traded goods such as jewelry
and glass.

Merchants sailed to eastern Africa, India, and
southeast Asia for goods not found in the empire.
Some traveled overland to China to buy silk, which
was prized for use in clothing. Romans used
currency to pay for goods. Roman coins were
made of gold and silver. Nearly everyone would
accept these coins.

> Why might nearly every trader
> have taken Roman coins?
> _____
> _____
> _____

THE PAX ROMANA

The **Pax Romana**, or Roman Peace, lasted about
200 years, until about AD 180. It was a time of
overall peace and prosperity. The empire's
population increased. Trade expanded and many
Romans became wealthy. The quality of life for
Romans and people in the provinces got better.
Many Romans were poor but could buy tickets to
events such as circuses, chariot races, and gladiator
fights. Roman baths were places of restful pleasure
and public conversations. Rome's public buildings
were beautiful.

> Use the library or an online
> resource to find out more about
> the life of the poor in Rome during
> the Pax Romana.

More people lived in the country than in Rome's
cities. Most country people farmed the land. They
grew enough food for their families. Many rural
people spoke languages other than Latin and kept
their own ways rather than following Roman
customs. **Villas** provided Rome's city dwellers with
a break from city life. In their country villas Romans
lived very much as they did in Rome. They had
large, fancy dinner parties. Slaves often worked in
villas and the surrounding fields. Selling crops from
the fields helped pay for the villa owners' expenses.

> How did most Romans in the
> country make their living?
> _____
> _____
> _____

CHALLENGE ACTIVITY

Critical Thinking: Evaluating You are traveling around the Roman
Empire. Write an essay evaluating city life and country life. **HSS
Analysis Skills HR 5**

The Roman Empire

MAIN IDEAS

1. The Romans looked for ways to use science and engineering to improve their lives.

2. Roman architecture and art were largely based on Greek ideas.

3. Roman literature and language have influenced how people write and speak.

4. Roman law serves as a model for modern law codes around the world.

 HSS 6.7

Students analyze the geographic, political, economic, religious, and social structures during the development of Rome.

Key Terms and People

Galen great Greek doctor who lived in the Roman Empire in the AD 100s

aqueduct raised channel used to carry water from the mountains into the cities

vault set of arches that supports the roof of a building

Ovid poet who wrote about Roman mythology

satire style of writing that pokes fun at people or society

Romance languages languages that developed from Latin, including Italian, French, Spanish, Portuguese, and Romanian

civil law legal system based on a written code of laws

Section Summary

ROMAN SCIENCE AND ENGINEERING

Unlike the Greeks, most Romans did not study the world just to learn about it. The Romans mainly wanted knowledge to help improve their lives. The Romans were practical. Their doctors studied the works of the Greeks, including **Galen**, to find ways of improving human health.

The Romans were skilled engineers and builders. They developed new materials, such as cement, so their structures would last. Examples of the Roman **aqueduct** still stand. The Romans used the **vault** to create large, open spaces within buildings. Roman buildings were bigger than any previously created.

> Why did the Romans mainly want to learn about the world?
>
> _____
>
> _____

> Why do you think some Roman structures still stand?
>
> _____
>
> _____

ARCHITECTURE AND ART

The Romans prized beauty as well as practical things. Roman architecture was greatly influenced by earlier Greek designs. The Romans used columns in public buildings to make them look grand, as the Greeks had done. However, Roman engineering allowed them to create much larger buildings, such as the Colosseum. This huge building was used to hold gladiator fights.

Beautiful mosaics covered many Roman floors. Frescoes, or paintings done on plaster, often decorated their walls. Many Roman sculptors copied the great Greek sculptures.

> Why might the Romans have copied Greek architecture?
>
> _____
>
> _____
>
> _____

LITERATURE AND LANGUAGE

Ovid wrote lovely poems and Virgil wrote a great epic, the *Aeneid,* about the founding of Rome. Romans excelled in **satire**, which has been a model for many modern works of literature. The Roman poets wrote in Latin, the language of ancient Rome. Latin greatly influenced the development of the **Romance languages**. Many Latin words are still used today in English. Some examples are *circus* and *veto*. Scientific naming systems and many mottoes are in the Latin language.

> Underline the Latin words used today in the English language.

LAW

Civil law was inspired by Roman law, which was enforced throughout the Roman Empire and continued to exist even after the empire fell apart. Most European nations today have civil law traditions.

> Why do you think civil law continues today in most of Europe?
>
> _____
>
> _____
>
> _____

CHALLENGE ACTIVITY

Critical Thinking: Rating In your opinion, which of the following was the greatest Roman contribution to today's world: engineering, architecture, poetry, or civil law? Write a brief speech defending your opinion. **HSS Analysis Skills HI 2**

Name _____ Class _____ Date _____

Rome and Christianity

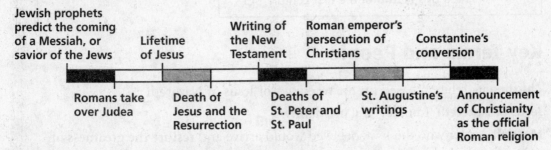

HISTORY–SOCIAL SCIENCE STANDARDS
HSS 6.7 Students analyze the geographic, political, economic, religious, and social structures during the development of Rome.
HSS Analysis HI 3 Explain the sources of historical continuity and how the combination of ideas and events explains the emergence of new patterns.

CHAPTER SUMMARY

Jewish prophets predict the coming of a Messiah, or savior of the Jews | Lifetime of Jesus | Writing of the New Testament | Roman emperor's persecution of Christians | Constantine's conversion

Romans take over Judea | Death of Jesus and the Resurrection | Deaths of St. Peter and St. Paul | St. Augustine's writings | Announcement of Christianity as the official Roman religion

COMPREHENSION AND CRITICAL THINKING

Use information from the graphic organizer to answer the following questions.

1. Explain Who was the Messiah? Why did Jews think he was important?

_____

_____

2. Identify Cause and Effect List at least one reason why Christianity spread so rapidly through the Roman Empire.

_____

_____

3. Evaluate Why do you think some Roman emperors feared and persecuted Christians?

_____

_____

4. Draw a Conclusion Why do you think Rome eventually adopted Christianity, which was once illegal in the Roman Empire, as Rome's official religion?

_____

_____

Rome and Christianity

Section 1

MAIN IDEAS

1. The Romans allowed many religions to be practiced in their empire.

2. Jews and Romans clashed over religious and political ideas.

3. The roots of Christianity had appeared in Judea by the end of the first century BC.

 HSS 6.7
Students analyze the geographic, political, economic, religious, and social structures during the development of Rome.

Key Terms and People

Christianity religion based on the teachings of Jesus of Nazareth

Jesus of Nazareth founder of Christianity

Messiah leader who the Jews believed would arrive and restore the greatness of David's ancient kingdom

Section Summary

ROMANS ALLOW MANY RELIGIONS

The Romans were a religious people. They believed in many gods. Because they did not know which gods were real, they prayed to all gods. The Romans usually allowed the people they conquered to keep their religious customs. Sometimes the Romans even adopted those customs, too. But if the Roman leaders thought a religion might cause a political problem, they would ban that religion. Roman leaders thought that Judaism was a political problem so they tried to stop it.

> Why did the Romans pray to so many gods?
> _____
> _____
> _____

JEWS AND ROMANS CLASH

Judea, the homeland for many Jews, was taken over by the Roman Empire in 63 BC. The Romans did not like Judaism for religious reasons. Jews worshipped only one god. Some Romans thought that this was insulting to all of their gods. Jews were allowed to practice their religion freely until they became a political problem.

> Why would some Romans find monotheism insulting?
> _____
> _____
> _____

Interactive Reader and Study Guide

The Jews did not want to be ruled by Rome so they started several rebellions. Roman emperor Hadrian got tired of putting down the rebellions so he banned some Jewish religious practices. Hadrian hoped that this would cause people to quit their religion, but it made the Jews more rebellious. Uprisings became more frequent. Eventually Rome destroyed Jerusalem, the capital city of Judea. The Jews were forced to leave and move to other countries with non-Jews. The Jews of Judea were scattered throughout the Roman Empire.

> **Do you think it was unwise of Hadrian to forbid Jewish religious practice? Why or why not?**
>
> _____
> _____
> _____

THE ROOTS OF CHRISTIANITY

During the beginning of the first century AD, a new religion appeared in Judea. This religion was **Christianity**. Chrisianity had its roots in Judaism, but was based on the teachings of **Jesus of Nazareth**.

When Jesus was born, there were several Jewish groups in Judea. The largest group of Jews followed the laws of Moses very strictly. Many of these Jews believed a new leader would appear among them. They believed that if they followed the rules, the leader would appear more quickly. This leader was called the **Messiah** (muh-SY-uh), which means "anointed" in the Hebrew language. For generations Jewish prophets had said that the Messiah would be a descendent of King David. They said that the Messiah would restore the greatness of David's ancient kingdom in Israel. When the Romans took over Judea, many Jews felt the Messiah would be coming soon.

> **Why do you think the Messiah was so important for the Jews who were living in Judea under Roman rule?**
>
> _____
> _____
> _____
> _____

CHALLENGE ACTIVITY

Critical Thinking: Drawing Inferences The Roman emperor Hadrian had his own way of dealing with a rebellious group of people. If you were Hadrian, would you do the same thing? Write a one-page paper discussing what you would do and why. **HSS Analysis Skills CR 1, CR 5, HI 1**

Rome and Christianity

MAIN IDEAS

1. In Christian belief, Jesus was the Messiah and the son of God.

2. Jesus taught about salvation, love for God, and kindness.

3. Jesus's followers, especially Paul, spread his teachings after his death.

 HSS 6.7

Students analyze the geographic, political, economic, religious, and social structures during the development of Rome.

Key Terms and People

Bible the holy book of Christianity

crucifixion a type of execution that involved being nailed to a cross

Resurrection the Christian belief that Jesus rose from the dead three days after his crucifixion

disciples followers

Apostles the 12 disciples whom Jesus chose to receive special teaching

Paul an early Christian disciple who preached Jesus's teachings throughout the Roman Empire and wrote letters defining Christianity as separate from Judaism

saint person known and admired for his or her holiness

Section Summary

THE LIFE AND DEATH OF JESUS OF NAZARETH

Jesus of Nazareth was born at the end of the first century BC. Much of what we know about Jesus is contained in the Christian **Bible**, the holy book of Christianity. The Christian Bible is made up of two parts. The first part is called the Old Testament, which is mostly the same as the Hebrew Bible. The second part, the New Testament, tells the story of Jesus and the early history of Christianity.

According to the Bible, Jesus was born in Bethlehem (BETH-li-hem) to a woman named Mary and her husband, Joseph, who was a carpenter. Christians believe that God, not Joseph, was the father of Jesus. When Jesus was about 30, he left his home in Nazareth to travel and teach. He gained many followers, but also made enemies.

> What is the primary source of information available about the life of Jesus of Nazareth?
>
> _____
>
> _____

The Roman leaders thought Jesus's teachings challenged their authority. Jesus was arrested and executed by **crucifixion**. Jesus was buried, but Christians believe he rose from the dead three days later. This is called the **Resurrection.** The Bible says that Jesus made many appearances to his **disciples**, or followers, during the next 40 days.

> Why do you think Jesus's teachings might have challenged the authority of the Roman leaders?
> _____
> _____
> _____
> _____

ACTS AND TEACHINGS

Jesus taught that people should treat others as you would like to be treated yourself. He also said that people should love God like a father. Jesus also taught about salvation, the rescue of people from sin. Jesus said that people who were saved from sin would enter the Kingdom of God when they died. Many people have interpreted Jesus's teachings in different ways. As a result, many different groups of Christians have been formed. However, Christians around the world share some basic beliefs about Jesus and his importance.

> Why have different groups of Christians formed?
> _____
> _____
> _____
> _____

JESUS'S FOLLOWERS

Jesus chose 12 of his disciples, the **Apostles**, to spread the message of Christianity. They were close friends and followers chosen and trained by Jesus himself. However, another man, **Paul**, was the most important figure in the spread of Christianity, although he never met Jesus. Paul traveled to many cities and wrote long letters explaining the meaning of Christianity. Paul did more than anyone else to spread Christian ideals. After he died, Paul was named a **saint**, a person known and admired for his or her holiness.

> Who was responsible for spreading Jesus's message?
> _____
> _____
> _____
> _____

CHALLENGE ACTIVITY

Critical Thinking: Drawing Inferences Do people today follow Jesus's teachings about being kind to others? Think of an event that you have read about or that you have experienced personally. Write a one-page paper discussing whether the people involved in that event followed the rules taught by Jesus. **HSS Analysis Skills CR 1, HI 3**

Rome and Christianity

Section 3

MAIN IDEAS
1. Christianity spread quickly in the Roman Empire, but its growing strength worried some emperors.
2. As the church grew, new leaders and ideas appeared and Christianity's status in the empire changed.

HSS 6.7.7
Students analyze the geographic, political, economic, religious, and social structures during the development of Rome.

Key Terms and People

martyrs people who die for their religious beliefs

persecution punishing people for their beliefs

bishops local Christian leaders

Eucharist the central ceremony of Christianity, celebrating Jesus's last meal

pope the bishop of Rome and leader of the church

Augustine of Hippo philosopher who applied the writings of Plato to the teachings of Jesus

Constantine Roman emperor who became a Christian

Section Summary

CHRISTIANITY SPREADS QUICKLY IN ROME

Apostles and teachers like Paul quickly spread the message of Christianity throughout the Roman Empire. As Christianity became more popular, Roman leaders began to worry. At first Jesus's followers had focused on converting only Jews. But soon, Christians began preaching to non-Jews. They offered copies of the gospels to everyone.

> Why do you think the early Christians were so slow to offer their message to non-Jews?
> _____
> _____
> _____
> _____

Some local leaders arrested and killed Christians. These Christians then became famous as **martyrs**, people who are killed for their religious beliefs. Saint Peter, an Apostle and the first bishop of Rome, and Saint Paul were killed for teaching Christianity. Some Roman emperors outlawed Christianity and **persecuted** Christians for their beliefs. Christians wore secret symbols, such as a fish, to identify each other.

> Underline the names of two famous Christian martyrs who died for their beliefs.

THE CHURCH GROWS

Because there was no central church, Christian teaching was left up to the **bishops**, or local Christian leaders. They would lead people in the **Eucharist**, the central ceremony of the Christian church. People would drink wine and eat bread to recall Jesus's last meal. By 200 AD, the bishops became more important, especially in the big cities. The most important bishop was the bishop of Rome, called the **pope**.

> **What was the Eucharist ceremony meant to honor?**
> _____
> _____

Slowly, Christianity became part of Roman society. Educated Christians began to see some similarities between Christianity and Greek and Roman philosophy. During the 300s AD, an influential Christian philospher, **Augustine of Hippo**, applied the ideas of Plato to Christianity. He stressed that Christians should focus on spiritual concerns instead of material things. His ideas helped shape Christian beliefs for hundreds of years.

The Roman Emperor **Constantine**, who came to power in 306, removed many restrictions on Christians. He created a Christian council to clarify the religion's teachings. Constantine himself soon became a Christian. As a result, the Christian religion became legitimate throughout the Roman Empire. Sixty years after Constantine's death, Christianity was declared the official religion of Rome.

> **Do you think the Romans continued to persecute Christians after Constantine's conversion? Why or why not?**
> _____
> _____
> _____
> _____

CHALLENGE ACTIVITY

Critical Thinking: Drawing Inferences Which person described in this chapter do you think had the greatest influence on the spread of Christianity? Write a one-page essay describing why this person was more important than other religious figures of the time. **HSS Analysis Skills CS 1, CR 5, HI 2**

The Fall of Rome

HISTORY–SOCIAL SCIENCE STANDARDS

HSS 7.1 Students analyze the causes and effects of the vast expansion and ultimate disintegration of the Roman Empire.
Analysis Skill HSS HI 4 Recognize the role of chance, oversight, and error in history.

CHAPTER SUMMARY

Tables of Similarities and Differences in the Roman Empire

	Western Empire	Eastern Empire
Capital		Constantinople
Religious leaders	popes and bishops	
Political leaders		emperor
Date of fall	476	
Conquered by		Ottoman Turks

COMPREHENSION AND CRITICAL THINKING

Use the answers to the following questions to fill in the graphic organizer above.

1. Explain Why was the Roman Empire divided into the east and the west?

_____

2. Identify Cause and Effect Why did the eastern empire last longer than the western empire?

_____

3. Evaluate Give at least two examples of how the people of the eastern empire were different than those in the western empire.

_____

4. Draw a Conclusion Would you have rather lived in the eastern empire or the western empire? Explain your answer.

_____

_____

The Fall of Rome

MAIN IDEAS

1. Many problems threatened the Roman Empire, leading one emperor to divide it in half.
2. Barbarians invaded Rome in the 300s and 400s.
3. Many factors contributed to Rome's fall.

 HSS 7.1

Students analyze the causes and effects of the vast expansion and ultimate disintegration of the Roman Empire.

Key Terms and People

Diocletian emperor who divided the Roman Empire into two parts

Clovis Frankish king who built a huge kingdom in Gaul

Attila fearsome Hun leader who attacked Rome's eastern empire

corruption decay in people's values

Section Summary

PROBLEMS THREATEN THE EMPIRE

At its height, the Roman Empire stretched from Britain south to Egypt, and from the Atlantic Ocean to the Persian Gulf. But by the end of the 100s, emperors had to give up much of that land. The empire was too big to manage well.

Rome had to defend itself constantly. Attacks came from Germany in the north and from Persia in the east. Problems came from within the empire, too. Disease killed many people. Taxes were high. Food was scarce because so many farmers went to war. To increase food production, German farmers were invited to work on Roman lands, but they were not loyal to Rome. Rebellions soon followed.

The emperor **Diocletian** took power in the late 200s. His solution to Rome's problems was to split the empire into two parts. Diocletian ruled the east. He appointed a co-emperor to rule the west. The Emperor Constantine briefly reunited the empire.

> Name three problems facing the Roman Empire around 200.
> _____
> _____
> _____
> _____

> Underline the clause that explains why the Roman Empire began running out of food.

> Do you think Diocletian's decision to divide the Roman Empire made sense? Why or why not?
> _____
> _____
> _____
> _____

Interactive Reader and Study Guide

He moved the capital from Rome to a new city he built in the east. He named the city Constantinople, which means "the city of Constantine."

BARBARIANS INVADE ROME

Once the capital moved to the eastern empire, German barbarians started more attacks on Roman territory in the north. During the late 300s, an Asian group called the Huns began attacking a group called the Goths. As the Huns pushed farther into Goth territory, the Goths were forced into Roman territory. Eventually the Goths penetrated deep into Italy and destroyed Rome.

After the destruction of Rome, more groups began invading Roman territory. The Angles, Saxons, and Jutes invaded Britain. The Franks invaded Gaul. The Frankish king **Clovis**, one of the most powerful German kings, built a large kingdom in Gaul. Meanwhile the east was menaced by a fearsome new Hun leader named **Attila**.

In 476 another barbarian leader overthrew the Roman emperor and declared himself king. This ended the western empire.

> Attila the Hun is one of the most notorious figures in history. Why do you think this is so?
>
> _____
> _____
> _____
> _____

FACTORS IN ROME'S FALL

Barbarian invasions were not the only causes of Rome's fall. The empire was too big, making it difficult to rule efficiently. The government also suffered from **corruption**. As these problems grew, wealthy landowners left Rome. They preferred to build armies and protect their personal estates. Only the poor were left in the city. Rome was no longer the great center it had once been.

> A famous phrase says "power corrupts." Do you think this is true? Why or why not?
>
> _____
> _____
> _____
> _____

CHALLENGE ACTIVITY

Critical Thinking: Drawing Inferences Was there anything Roman rulers could have done to stop the disintegration of the western empire or was its fall inevitable? Write a one-page essay explaining your answer.
HSS Analysis Skills CS 1, HR 5, HI 1

The Fall of Rome

MAIN IDEAS

1. Eastern emperors ruled from Constantinople and tried but failed to reunite the whole Roman Empire.

2. The people of the eastern empire created a new society that was very different from society in the west.

3. Byzantine Christianity was different from religion in the west.

 HSS 7.1
Students analyze the causes and effects of the vast expansion and ultimate disintegration of the Roman Empire.

Key Terms and People

Justinian last ruler of the Roman Empire

Theodora Justinian's wife, a wise woman who advised her husband during his reign

Byzantine Empire civilization that developed in the eastern Roman Empire

mosaics pictures made with pieces of colored glass and stone

Section Summary

EMPERORS RULE FROM CONSTANTINOPLE

Constantinople lay between the Black Sea and Mediterranean Sea. This location between the two seas protected Constantinople from attack and helped the city control trade between Europe and Asia. As Rome fell, Constantinople grew.

Constantinople is now called Istanbul. Find its location in a world atlas. Why do you think it developed as a major trade center?

_____

_____

_____

_____

Justinian, an eastern emperor who took power in the 500s, wanted to reunite the Roman Empire. His armies managed to recapture Italy. He earned respect for updating, simplifying, and writing down Roman laws, making them more fair. But he made enemies who tried to overthrow him. Justinian got advice from his wife **Theodora**, and was able to stop the riots and keep his throne.

Who was Justinian's advisor?

_____

_____

Despite Justinian's success, later emperors could not fight off barbarian attacks or hold onto the land. The eastern empire lasted for another 700 years after Justianian's death, but Constantinople was conquered by the Ottoman Turks in 1453.

A NEW SOCIETY

Justinian is considered the last Roman emperor. After Justinian's death, people in the eastern empire began to follow Greek culture instead of Roman culture. The cultural ties to Rome were slowly lost.

Constantinople was a major trade route among Europeans, Africans, and Asians. Because of this, the people of Constantinople were exposed to new ideas from other cultures. They blended those ideas with their own Roman and Greek roots. Historians call the new society that developed in the east the **Byzantine Empire**. Byzantine culture developed its own distinct features. An eastern emperor, for example, was head of both the church and the government. In the west, popes and bishops ruled the church, but the emperor held political power.

> Why is Justinian considered the "last Roman emperor?"
> _____
> _____
> _____
> _____

BYZANTINE CHRISTIANITY

Christianity was central to the Byzantine Empire. It was illegal to practice any other religion. Artwork dealt with religious themes. Byzantine artists of the period are know for making spectacular **mosaics**, pictures that are made from pieces of colored glass and stone.

For hundreds of years the church leaders of the east and west worked together. Shortly after 1000, the church split in two. Christians in the east formed what is known as the Eastern Orthodox Church. This religious division opened a huge cultural gap between eastern and western Europe.

> Underline the name of the only legally practiced religion in the Byzantine Empire.

> Some historians believe that the well-known historical division between the "eastern" and "western" worlds begins in Byzantine culture. Do you think this so? Why or why not?
> _____
> _____
> _____
> _____
> _____

CHALLENGE ACTIVITY

Critical Thinking: Drawing Inferences Imagine that you are Theodora, the wife of Roman Emperor Justinian. You think your husband is making a mistake when he says he wants to leave his kingdom because his enemies have started a riot and threaten to kill him. As a woman you have no power to rule the land. So how would you persuade him to stay and solve the problems with his enemies? Write your answer in the style of a verbal appeal, or speech, you would make to Justinian. **HSS Analysis Skills CR 1, CR 5, HI 4**

The Early Americas

HISTORY–SOCIAL SCIENCE STANDARDS
HSS 7.7 Students compare and contrast the geographic, political, economic, religious, and social structures of the Meso-American and Andean civilizations.
HSS Analysis Skill HR3 Distinguish relevant from irrelevant, essential from incidental, and verifiable from unverifiable information.

CHAPTER SUMMARY

The domestication of maize	led to	settled life in Mesoamerica
The rise of villages and towns	led to	the development of a trading network
The growth of cities	led to	new discoveries in science, math, and writing
Warfare and drought	led to	the collapse of the Maya civilization

COMPREHENSION AND CRITICAL THINKING

Use information from the graphic organizer to answer the following questions.

1. **Explain** What and where was the first domesticated crop grown in Mesoamerica?

_____

2. **Identify Cause and Effect** How did the domestication of corn change the lives of the early Americans?

_____

3. **Evaluate** How did the Maya show their respect for corn?

_____

_____

4. **Draw a Conclusion** How did the growth cycle of corn influence our modern concept of a 365-day year?

_____

_____

The Early Americas

MAIN IDEAS

1. The geography of the Americas is varied with a wide range of landforms.
2. The first people to arrive in the Americas were hunter-gatherers.
2. The development of farming led to early settlement in the Americas.

 HSS 7.7.1

Students compare and contrast the geographic, political, economic, religious, and social structures of the Meso-American and Andean civilizations.

Key Terms and People

Mesoamerica region that includes the southern part of what is now Mexico and parts of the northern countries of Central America

maize corn

Section Summary

GEOGRAPHY OF THE AMERICAS

The Americas are made up of two continents, North America and South America. These continents have a wide range of landforms. The first people of the Americas were hunter-gatherers. They depended on the geography of the land to find food.

Historians call the cultural region in the southern part of North America **Mesoamerica**. Mesoamerica extended from the middle of modern-day Mexico south to Central America. The region's many rain forests and rivers created fertile farmland. The first farmers in the Americas domesticated plants there.

> Underline the description of the land included in the area called Mesoamerica.

THE FIRST PEOPLE ARRIVE

No one is sure how people first arrived in the Americas. Some scientists believe they came from Asia some time before 12,000 BC, walking over a land bridge that crossed the Bering Strait. Other historians think the first Americans arrived by sea.

The earliest people were hunter-gatherers. These people survived on wild buffalo and other animals,

> Fill in the blanks: Some scientists believe the first Americans arrived by
>
> _____
>
> while others believe they arrived by
>
> _____
>
> _____

Interactive Reader and Study Guide

as well as fruits, nuts, and wild grains. They moved
frequently, depending upon where food was most
plentiful. Some people eventually settled along the
coastal areas, fishing and planting different types of
seeds to see which would grow best. This changed
early American life.

> Circle the main factor that
> changed life in the early Americas.

FARMING AND SETTLEMENT

The experiments with seeds led to farming. This
allowed people to live in one place permanently.
The first farming settlements were in Mesoamerica.
By 3500 BC Mesoamericans were growing **maize**, or
corn. Later they learned to grow squash and beans.
As in other areas of the world, once people settled,
towns and cities were created. The population grew
and societies began to develop religion, art, and
trade opportunities.

> Why does experimenting with
> seeds lead to farming?
> _____
> _____
> _____
> _____

Historians believe that the Olmec (OHL-mek)
were the first Mesoamericans to live in villages.
Some Olmec lived in bigger towns, which were the
centers of government and religion. They built
pyramids and huge stone sculptures of their rulers
and gods. They developed a large trading network.

Archaeological evidence suggests the Olmec
may have created the first written language in
the Americas and designed a calendar. Later
civilizations that traded with the Olmec were
influenced by Olmec culture. Other civilizations
developed in South America around farming. The
methods for growing maize spread throughout
South and North America.

> What Olmec achievement had the
> most lasting effect on American
> civilizations?
> _____
> _____

CHALLENGE ACTIVITY

Critical Thinking: Drawing Inferences Draw a timeline showing how
the first human civilization developed in the Americas. Start with the
two theories of how humans first arrived to the Americas, and end with
the establishment of the Olmec civilization. **HSS Analysis Skills HR 3,
HR 5, HI 4**

MAIN IDEAS
1. Geography affected early Maya civilization.
2. The Maya Classic Age was characterized by great cities, trade, and warfare.
3. Maya civilization declined, and historians have several theories as to why.

 HSS 7.7
Students compare and contrast the geographic, political, economic, religious, and social structures of the Meso-American and Andean civilizations.

Key Terms and People

obsidian a sharp, glasslike volcanic rock found in Mesoamerica

Pacal Maya king who dedicated a temple to record his achievements as ruler

Section Summary

GEOGRAPHY AFFECTS EARLY MAYA

The Maya (MY-uh) civilization developed in the lowlands of Mesoamerica around 1000 BC. Thick forests covered the area, so the Maya had to cut down trees to farm. The forest was also a source of many resources, including animals for food and wood for building materials.

   The Maya lived in villages. The Maya began trading such items as woven cloth and **obsidian**, a sharp, glasslike volcanic rock. By AD 200 the Maya were building the first large cities in the Americas.

> **Circle the approximate date that Maya civilization developed in the Mesoamerican lowlands.**

MAYA CLASSIC AGE

Maya civilization reached its height between AD 250 and 900, a period called the Classic Age. During this time there were more than more than 40 Maya cities. Each city had populations of 5,000 to 50,000 people. The Maya traded for things that could not be found in their own part of Mesoamerica. The lowlands had many crops and wood products. The highlands had valuable stones like jade and obsidian.

   The Maya built large stone pyramids, temples, and palaces. Some of these buildings honored

> **List three valued Maya exports.**
>
> _____
>
> _____
>
> _____

local kings. A temple built in the city of Palenque (pah-LENG-kay) honored the king **Pacal** (puh-KAHL). Artists decorated the temple with paintings and carvings celebrating his achievements as ruler. The Maya built canals to bring water to the cities. They shaped hillsides into flat terraces so they could grow crops on them. The Maya also paved the cities' central plazas. Most cities had a ball court to watch a game the Maya had learned from the Olmec.

> **How do historians know about the rule of the Maya king Pacal?**
> _____
> _____
> _____
> _____

The Maya did not have a central government. Kings governed each city separately. Cities often fought each other over territory and resources. This warfare was violent and destructive. Some historians believe warfare led to the end of the Maya civilization.

> **Do you think a central government might have saved Maya civilization? Why or why not?**
> _____.
> _____
> _____
> _____

MAYA CIVILIZATION DECLINES

Maya civilization began to collapse in the 900s. They stopped building large buildings and left the cities for the countryside. Historians are not sure why this happened, but there are several theories.

Some historians believe that Maya farmers kept planting the same crop over and over, which weakened the soil and caused drought. This may have caused more competition and war between the cities. Others think that the Maya kings made their people build huge temples or farm for them. The people got tired of working for the kings, so they rebelled. There were probably many factors that led to the decline of the Maya civilization.

> **List two factors that may have contributed to the decline of the Maya civilization.**
> _____
> _____
> _____

CHALLENGE ACTIVITY

Critical Thinking: Drawing Inferences One of the sources of information that historians have about the Maya comes from Maya kings like Pacal, who dedicated an entire temple to his achievements. If you were to dedicate a building to honor your life, what would it look like? Draw a picture of a building, including paintings and carvings that might be included on the walls. Think about what would be helpful to historians in the future who might want to reconstruct early 21st century life. **HSS Analysis Skills CS 3, CR 3, HI 5**

The Early Americas

MAIN IDEAS

1. Roles in Maya society were based on a complex class structure.
2. Religion in Maya society was often bloody.
3. The Maya made achievements in art, science, math, and writing.

 HSS 7.7

Students compare and contrast the geographic, political, economic, religious, and social structures of the Meso-American and Andean civilizations.

Key Terms and People

observatories buildings designed to study astronomy and view the stars

Popol Vuh a book containing legends and some history of the Maya civilization

Section Summary

ROLES IN MAYA SOCIETY

The Maya had a complex social structure. The upper and lower classes led very different lives. Kings held the highest position. Priests, warriors, and merchants made up the upper class.

> Underline the names of the groups who made up the upper classes of Maya society.

The Maya believed that their rulers were related to the gods. Men and women could be rulers, but they had to have been born into a royal family. Priests were also born into their roles. Priests were highly educated. They used their knowledge of astronomy and mathematics to plan religious ceremonies. The warriors fought the battles and the merchants directed trade. Together, these four groups controlled political, economic, and religious life for the Maya.

Most Maya belonged to lower-class farming families. They lived in little houses outside the cities. Girls were taught to run the household. Men hunted and farmed. Maya farmers were required to serve the upper class. They had to give up some of their crops and make goods for the upper class. They were also used as labor to build temples. Slaves held the lowest position in Maya society.

> List three ways in which Maya farmers served the upper class.
>
> _____
> _____
> _____
> _____
> _____

Section 3, *continued*

RELIGION

The Maya worshipped many gods. They believed that each god represented a different area of life. The Maya believed that their kings spoke with the gods.

The Maya believed the gods could either help them or hurt them, so they tried to keep the gods happy. They thought that the gods needed blood, so everyone gave blood by piercing their skin or tongue. Special rituals of blood giving were held at births, weddings, and funerals. On special occasions the Maya believed the gods needed extra amounts of blood. They made human sacrifices to the gods.

> What did the Maya think their gods wanted in order to be appeased?
>
> _____
>
> _____

ACHIEVEMENTS

Maya achievements in art, architecture, math, science, and writing were remarkable. They did not have metal tools or wheeled vehicles, but they built huge stone structures. They are known for their stone carvings and jade and gold jewelry.

More important, though, are the advances the Maya made in astronomy and the development of the modern calendar. They built **observatories** for their priests to study the stars. They learned that the year had about 365 days. They developed a number system to go along with their calendar and record important events in their history.

> What did the Maya use their special numbering system for?
>
> _____
>
> _____
>
> _____

The Maya also developed a writing system similar to Egyptian hieroglyphics. They wrote on bark paper and carved records onto stone tablets. After the Spanish arrived, the legends and history of the Maya were written in a book called the **Popol Vuh** (poh-pohl voo).

> Underline the phrase that describes the contents of the Popol Vuh.

CHALLENGE ACTIVITY

Critical Thinking: Drawing Inferences You are a Maya astronomer. List the twelve months of the year. Then under each month, write three astronomical events that might indicate a repeated cycle.

HSS Analysis Skills CS 3, HI 6